Crafting

Ethnography

Crafting

Ethnography

Paul Atkinson

◎SAGE

Los Angeles | London | New Delhi
Singapore | Washington DC | Melbourne

⑤SAGE

SAGE Publications Ltd
1 Oliver's Yard
55 City Road
London EC1Y 1SP

SAGE Publications Inc.
2455 Teller Road
Thousand Oaks, California 91320

SAGE Publications India Pvt Ltd
B 1/I 1 Mohan Cooperative Industrial Area
Mathura Road
New Delhi 110 044

SAGE Publications Asia-Pacific Pte Ltd
3 Church Street
#10-04 Samsung Hub
Singapore 049483

Editor: Alysha Owen
Editorial assistant: Hannah Cavender-Deere
Senior project editor: Chris Marke
Project management: TNQ Technologies
Marketing manager: Ben Sherwood
Cover design: Shaun Mercier
Typeset by: TNQ Technologies

Library of Congress Control Number: 2021942571

British Library Cataloguing in Publication data

A catalogue record for this book is available from the
British Library

ISBN 978-1-5297-0123-4
ISBN 978-1-5297-0122-7 (pbk)

Contents

About the Author

Paul Atkinson is Emeritus Professor of Sociology at Cardiff University. Recent publications include *Ethnographic Engagements*, with Sara Delamont (Routledge 2021), and *Reflexivity and Social Research*, with Emilie Morwenna Whitaker (Palgrave 2021). The previous books in this quartet were *For Ethnography* (SAGE 2014), *Thinking Ethnographically* (SAGE 2017) and *Writing Ethnographically* (SAGE 2019). The fourth edition of Hammersley and Atkinson *Ethnography: Principles in Practice* was published by Routledge in 2019. He was a co-editor of the SAGE *Foundations of Social Research Methods*. He is a Fellow of the Academy of Social Sciences and of the Learned Society of Wales.

Acknowledgements

I must thank the highly talented people who let me spend time in their studios, and who taught me some elementary aspects of their art. The following appear in this book: Peter Layton and his colleagues at London Glassblowing, my teacher Layne Rowe in particular; Chris Keenan, potter; Nic Webb, woodworker; Ellie Swinhoe, silversmith and jewellery maker; Ion Paciu, photographer; Rachel Clark, artist; and Emmanuelle Moeglin, perfumer. Several others have generously given me time and allowed me to observe them at work, although I have not included them in this particular book: Sara Lee, printer; Howard Fenn, silversmith; and his studio colleagues.

I am, as always, grateful to present and past members of the Cardiff Ethnography Group, among them my co-authors: Emilie Whitaker, Katie Featherstone, William Housley, Robin Smith, Jamie Lewis and Neil Stephens. I have learned much from our collaborations.

My long-suffering editors at SAGE, Mila Steele and Alysha Owen, have helped me in shaping this book, and the previous three books in my quartet.

Much of the manuscript was typed by Rosemary Bartle-Jones, who is a genius at deciphering handwriting.

As ever, my gratitude to Sara Delamont is unbounded; she is my best friend and my best critic. She has put up with me and my drafts for over fifty years.

1

Ethnographic Instances

This book completes a quartet that began with *For Ethnography* (2015a) and continued with *Thinking Ethnographically* (2017) and *Writing Ethnographically* (2020). There has been a progression: the books have become more personal, having started with a very general manifesto-like overview of ethnography as an approach to social research. In other ways, the books have come full circle. *For Ethnography* is imbued with the imperative to *do* fieldwork, and with the activity of ethnographic analysis. In this last book of the quartet, the emphasis is again on doing. It is devoted to ethnographic investigations of making, and on the making of ethnography. At its root, therefore, this book is practical – about making things and doing ethnography. Too much methodological writing is at a level of abstraction that provides little guidance or exemplification as to how fieldwork is conducted in practice. Texts can offer little sense of how ethnographers transform their participation and their observations into textual reconstructions. My concern with practical ethnographic working means that I aim to demonstrate by example how we can take the materials we generate 'in the field' and *make* something of them. To a considerable extent, these books are an affirmation of what may seem to be rather traditional approaches to ethnographic research. While I am not inimical to innovation and change, I do believe that fundamental principles deserve to be respected: see Atkinson, Delamont and Housley (2008).

This discussion is based on a series of exercises that I have undertaken. I do not claim that they add up to and constitute a sustained 'research' programme. Rather, they should be thought of as methodological exercises. They were undertaken in order to explore aspects of embodied, carnal sociology; to explore aspects of sensory ethnography; to reflect on how ethnographers set about learning new things. They were all – as I shall describe shortly – brief attempts on my part to learn and to practise a variety of activities. Undertaken over a period of years, the exercises are used to develop some arguments about ethnographic participation, the nature of the phenomena we study and the practicalities of learning. In summary, I have taken introductory classes in the following activities: glass-blowing, silversmithing, woodworking, ceramics, perfume-blending, life-drawing and digital photography. Before embarking on my explicitly methodological activities, I had also taken classes in Argentine tango. I made detailed field notes about each of these activities. So they are not just examples of a retired academic's bucket list of leisure activities. I acknowledge that taking classes in things like ceramics is exactly the sort of thing that (mostly) middle-class people get up to in their leisure time, and classes exist to satisfy the curiosity and enthusiasm of amateurs, enthusiasts and hobbyists. People make presents of such classes for family members by way of gift vouchers, while other participants are craftworkers and hobbyists trying out a new medium or brushing up their skills. There are many craft classes for amateurs and enthusiasts in a wide range of arts and crafts. I have taken a series of classes in trying to understand some processes of learning and doing new things. Beyond their intrinsic interest and the potential enjoyment of those learning activities, my pursuit of them has had a serious side. I use them to illustrate some basic ideas about craft, skill, learning, the senses and the body. Such practical exercises might be likened – not too pompously, I hope – to the regular classes and exercises taken by performers and artists: the daily studio classes and exercises for dancers, the musician's scales and practice, the singer's regular voice coaching, the artist's sketchbooks and so on. Having reached a certain age, I can indulge in these activities, having the necessary time and money. Towards the end of a career, we can regain the relative freedom of the graduate student, with time and opportunity to pursue curiosity-driven enquiries.

Some brief remarks about these exercises are in order. The classes on which I base the following chapters are short introductory encounters. I do not claim to have mastered any of the activities I describe. That would entail a very different approach. It would imply a very long-term immersion, in the form of a protracted apprenticeship in just one craft. As I shall acknowledge later, there are plenty of examples of such long-term fieldwork, and I make no claim to have emulated the level of skill and expertise that prolonged fieldwork might yield. In some ways, of course, my own exercises run counter to the kind of ethnographic imagination that I have advocated for many years. That is, fieldwork that is intensive and extensive, conducted over time through a thorough engagement with a chosen setting (or multiple settings). Now I still believe that prolonged immersion – or a series of immersions – is the best kind of ethnographic research in most cases. It has been the hallmark of ethnographic fieldwork for over a century. Social worlds take time: it takes time to make sense of them, to observe the right sort of variety of events and routines and to participate in the rhythms and cycles of everyday life. Nothing has changed that methodological imperative. On the other hand, it is possible that we practitioners and methodologists have simply made too much of long-term immersive fieldwork. Sometimes we need to stop and ask ourselves how much fieldwork is really necessary. How many times do we really need to observe some routine activity in order to establish *that* it is routine, *how* it is accomplished and *why* it persists in that form. Conversely, how many ethnographers find themselves obsessively collecting 'data' that turn out to be overwhelming, so that much of what was observed and recorded goes unreported? Proverbially, graduate students collect far more information than they can really assimilate, analyse or report. So too do many more experienced researchers.

By contrast, I want to explore the value of what I call an *aliquot* of fieldwork. An aliquot is a small, unmeasured quantity that is deemed to be just enough for the task in hand. So one might be instructed to add to a solution an aliquot of a solvent – just sufficient to dissolve the ingredients. In the same spirit, I explore the idea of an *aliquot of fieldwork*. That is, small amounts (time not precisely defined) of fieldwork that are 'just enough' for one's research purposes. This recalls, in a slightly different form, the observation once made to me by Harry Wolcott, the anthropologist. He acknowledged that in the course of his career, he had only ever studied one of anything at a time: one village, one village school, one school principal. 'People ask me', he would say 'Harry, what on earth can you learn from just one?' and he would tell them, he said, 'As much as I can'. I do think that is a memorable lesson. In summary, I believe that one should sometimes try to learn a lot from a little, rather than always learning a little from a lot. Doing so entails the recognition that field 'data' (such as our field notes) are not just accumulated information, but are prompts towards our ethnographic thinking. Letting 'data' pile up, and then mounting a major assault on them in the name of 'analysis', is not the ideal way to proceed. Even if we undertake longer-term fieldwork, we all need to think clearly as we go along – and that involves trying to derive as many ideas as possible from relatively small amounts of fieldwork as we go along. In fact, in retrospect, I realise how often long-term fieldwork is actually episodic, with bursts of participation and observation interspersed with periods of writing and reflection.

This is not a completely original approach. There have been several commentaries on short-term (Pink and Morgan 2013) or focused (Knoblauch 2005) ethnography. None of those is an argument for doing short ethnographic fieldwork *instead of* longer-term immersion in a given social world. Rather, I encourage recognition of the value of shorter interventions for specific purposes. Knoblauch makes clear his use of 'focused' in this context. Short periods of participation and observation, accompanied by the collection of audio-visual data, permit a concentration on highly specific, often specialised, activities. Sociological ethnography is conducted in highly differentiated societies and can make no claim to 'holism' is describing a given 'culture'. At the same time, studies of more specific sites and practices have become more widely conducted. As Knoblauch (2005, para. 28) suggests, 'Focused ethnography …restricts itself to certain aspects of fields. The entities studied in focused ethnographies are not necessarily groups, organisations or milieus but rather situations, interactions and activities…'. In a similar vein, Streeck and Mehus (2005) describe 'microethnography' in terms of a focus on practices. Pink and Morgan include a focus on 'detail' as a characteristic of short-term fieldwork, a perspective that informs my own incursions into various sites of craft and artistic activity. I would only expand that to be: detailed attention to the practical activities of making and doing.

In addition to collecting too much information, many researchers act as if their work were entirely a matter of inductive inference. The implicit model seems to be: collect large volumes of data, and then apply various kinds of procedures in order to generate something that can be called 'analysis'. Those procedural approaches go under several labels. The most commonly used is Grounded Theory (GT), or at least a thoroughly vulgarised version of it. In its original formulation, GT was a general heuristic perspective concerned with the productive interaction between ideas, research design and sociological ideas (concepts). It recommended a highly active, exploratory dialogue between 'data' and 'ideas' in the pursuit of 'theory'. It was, in its original formulation, an approach that advocated an abductive approach to sociological inference (Tavory and Timmermans 2014). It was by no means confined to 'qualitative' research – although in subsequent discussion and use, it is widely assumed to relate exclusively to qualitative work. In its vulgar versions, the abductive character has been abandoned, in favour of a purely inductive one. To put it simply, the underlying model assumes a substantial volume of 'data' (field notes or interview transcripts) that are then inspected and coded in the search for recurrent themes. Although the advocates of it try to distance themselves from GT, so-called Thematic Analysis (TA) is very similar in that respect. It is predicated on the coding of (usually) large amounts of data – like GT, it is often based on a corpus of interview transcripts – through a series of analytic steps. Both GT and TA, in practice, look like rather laborious exercises in content analysis. My attempts at an aliquot of fieldwork are partly intended to counteract such crude and misleading perspectives. Small amounts of fieldwork invite intensive thinking. As I have already suggested, they can promote the attempt to learn 'as much as we can' from relatively brief incursions into the field.

Classes on how to throw a pot, how to blow glass or how to work in silver or wood were new for me personally, but they are not radically different from my previous sociological commitments. There is a direct continuity in some respects. Nearly all of my research has been about the creation and reproduction of knowledge and expert performances. That interest goes back to my doctoral research in the late 1960s, and to subsequent fieldwork in a similar vein in the 1980s. In both instances, I was preoccupied with the construction and performance of medical knowledge. A very brief recapitulation is in order. My doctoral research – my first sustained period of participant observation – was conducted in a medical school (Atkinson 1981). In particular, I focused on one of the most distinctive aspects of medical education – bedside teaching. The teaching round on a hospital ward has a long history. I observed its workings in the Edinburgh teaching hospitals, where the conduct of bedside instruction had historical links to the earliest years of modern medicine. In essence, I tried to document two key aspects of clinical instruction. First, I showed how the 'classic' aspects of medical knowledge were being reproduced in the hospital, that is, the categories of disease entities and their characteristic signs, the methods of clinical examination (observation, auscultation, palpation) and the transmission of such clinical knowledge. The process was, it transpired, based on clinicians' dramaturgical skills. Medicine is *performed* at the bedside. Teaching rounds, migrating from patient to patient on a hospital ward, and conducted by a clinician with a group of students, can consist of a series of dramatic enactments whereby the signs and symptoms of medical conditions are revealed. The medical categories of disease are thus displayed to the neophytes. From a personal point of view, as an ethnographer, such dramatic performances meant that – by virtue of my attentive presence at the bedside – I was exposed to a great many vivid enactments of medical knowledge. Even had I resisted it, I would have acquired a good deal of firsthand knowledge of clinical medicine. And of course I did not resist it. Indeed, it is one of the most characteristic features of clinical instruction that 'bedside' instruction furnishes vivid and highly memorable exemplars. Medical students and ethnographers alike find individual 'cases' strikingly memorable. If you witness the dramatic presentation of classic cases and classic symptoms, then it is virtually impossible not to assimilate at least some of those cases and their key features. Indeed, by following medical students in general medicine and surgery for two years, I observed much of their initial introduction to hospital medicine. I learned the ways of the clinic and of clinical medicine alongside the students.

Of course I do not, and have never, claimed to have acquired the same depth or breadth of knowledge as a full-time medical student. It would be hubris to do so, stupid and misleading. Rather, the fact is that an ethnographer who is attentive to the specialised knowledge of a given domain can, and should, become well versed in some aspects of that esoteric knowledge. There is, in other words, no question of the ethnographer standing aloof, refusing any such engagement in the interests of making things 'strange', or for fear of 'going native'. This is a theme that I shall return to in the course of the book. For now, I simply want to reaffirm the basic point: that through ethnographic engagement, one learns at least something of the local – often esoteric – knowledge that is in play. My own interest in and appreciation of medical knowledge was recapitulated and intensified when I undertook fieldwork among haematologists in the United States and in the United Kingdom (Atkinson 1995). Again, my interest was in the performance of medical knowledge and authority, focusing on haematologists' representations of their 'cases', and how disorders of the blood (such as leukaemia, aplastic anaemia or thrombocytopenia) are constructed. It was, and would have been, impossible to make sense of the dense cycle of rounds, clinical conferences and consultations without gaining some basic working knowledge of how blood is understood (cell lines, bleeding time, clotting factors), how they are investigated (peripheral blood smears, bone marrow aspirates or cell counts) and how the evidence is assembled to arrive at diagnoses, management decisions or advice to other clinicians (such as surgeons). In addition to attending and recording speech events such as clinical rounds and conferences, I paid close attention to sources that the haematologists themselves might use: text books, journal articles and atlases of clinical pathology. I gained elementary knowledge of conditions, their investigation and treatment.

A comparable interest in the enactment of medical expertise is visible in the work a group of us conducted in collaboration with medical geneticists. Amongst other topics, we studied how clinicians describe and identify the types and categories of the types and categories of *dysmorphology* (problems of abnormal development, resulting in a variety of distinctive physical appearance, behaviour and cognitive impairment). We focused especially on how experts generate such clinical assessments, and how they adjudicate the different types of evidence available to them (Latimer et al. 2006; Featherstone and Atkinson 2011). Such a sociological exercise on the sociology of medical knowledge likewise necessitates some degree of acquaintance with the classificatory schemata of genetic medicine. My understanding and analysis of clinical encounters would have been jejune without the acquisition of some level of understanding. Self-evidently, I was not trying to emulate the professionals, or to 'become' a medical practitioner. Equally, I was not trying to participate in their practical work. It is one thing to observe surgical teaching, but one cannot 'have a go' at performing surgery. That level of technical engagement would be unthinkable. Much of this book, on the other hand, *is* based on the practical activity of learning and doing, on the elementary acquisition of some basic competence.

My ethnographic encounters with specialised domains of performance and skill later led me to a study of the Welsh National Opera Company (Atkinson 2006a, b, c). While my fieldwork encompassed rather more settings, I devoted much of my time and attention to the rehearsal studio as well as rehearsals and performances in the theatre. While it would be perfectly possible to study some aspects of such events with no knowledge of or interest in opera as a performing art, it would have been a very difficult – and diminished – fieldwork exercise. Like clinical medicine, music theatre is an intensely *absorbing* social world. Each opera is rehearsed for a period of six weeks or so, and each new production brings together a different, unique team of performers, directors, designers and others, together with the employees of the Company. And for the period of time during which they collectively work on the production, they are intensely focused on getting things right. They have to get things right musically, and they have to get the dramatic performance right, too. Music and action have to come together: there is a great deal of coordination to be managed. That involves repetition. Rehearsals are by their very nature repetitive events. Indeed, repetition is a recurrent feature of many domains of performance and skill. A distinguished colleague once asked me, while I was doing my operatic fieldwork, what were the similarities between medical education and opera rehearsals. I replied 'Doing things over and over until they get them right'. It was a snap response, but there was more than a grain of truth, and repetition is something that runs through the contents of this book (which I hope nevertheless will not be unduly repetitious in itself).

The opera fieldwork also led to a small project on masterclasses for young opera singers, with Richard Watermeyer and Sara Delamont (Atkinson, Delamont and Watermeyer 2012; Atkinson 2013a, b). Like many such classes, they were intensely focused encounters, during which a highly experienced performer works closely with a younger singer. It is an exercise in repetition and expert commentary. The young singer performs the piece through, then that performance is commented on, the young singer being interrupted and made to repeat and modify aspects of the performance. Like the medical encounters I observed, these events are enactments of expertise and personal authority, as are the opera rehearsals, where the director and the conductor represent personal, embodied authority (Atkinson 2006b). So too were the medical collegial and instructional encounters I had worked on, where senior physicians perform expertise and express their expert opinions (Atkinson 1995).

In those settings, therefore, my ethnographic observations have embraced performance, enactment and embodiment. I have written about the local reproduction of skill and knowledge, technique and interpretation. While I have actively engaged intellectually with those esoteric domains, my observations have not been thoroughly participant observation. I was able to be present – to walk the wards, to sit in on rehearsals and so on – but there was little opportunity to try things out. In the medical school, I observed in the Anatomy dissecting room, but, of course, I did not try my hand at dissection, any more than I tried out examining patients or carrying out surgery. While among the haematologists, I did not practise phlebotomy, although I was able to observe blood smears under the microscope. Among the opera singers, I could not 'join in', although the gentlemen of the chorus occasionally teased me by suggesting that I should. I have never been able to sing in tune, so it would have been out of the question, even if the invitation had been a serious one.

In this book, I continue my abiding interest in practical knowledge, skill and technique. It also continues my recurrent interest in education – in the broadest of senses. From medical education to opera master classes, my analyses have included an interest in the embodied, personal authority of teachers. The substantive focus in this book shifts, while remaining fixed on topics of skill, technique and embodied performance. The overarching theme can be summarised as *craft* and *technique*, although as we shall see it encompasses a wide range of settings and activities. While there is continuity, there is also change from most of my previous fieldwork studies. In this portfolio of fieldwork encounters, I undertake only very short incursions into a 'field'. The various activities I have undertaken do not deserve the title of 'research', and they barely merit the designation of 'ethnography' either. They are possible because, having retired, I needed no research grant or official study leave in order to conduct fieldwork or to undertake the writing. For most purposes, ethnographic research, even shorter-term focused work, needs time, and 'time out' from the normal round of teaching and administration. Freedom to do such curiosity-led, methodological exercises is a luxury.

As I have already indicated, these exercises are *not* an argument against long-term, immersive fieldwork. Such ethnographic commitment remains the ideal for many studies. In the most general terms, one needs time for events to develop and unfold, and if one could conduct a 'proper' ethnography in a short space of time, then more of us would do so. So make no mistake: this is not an argument to the contrary. On the other hand, length of fieldwork and the accumulation of 'data' are not virtues in themselves. There is certainly no merit in amassing mountains of field notes, interview transcripts or documents if they are not subsequently made to yield interesting ideas. There is a cultural imperative, it would appear, to collect far too many data, which are then subjected to superficial analysis. Too often we are presented with 'thin' versions of 'analysis' (often based on interview transcripts rather than on observations) that do not do full justice to the content and organisation of actions (which can include speech acts). Although it is not the place here to engage in a sustained discussion, one finds too many textbooks and journal papers advocating things like GT or TA that – especially in over-simplified or vulgarised form – seem to result in a glorified version of content analysis. The data are 'coded' and sorted according to more or less sensitively defined categories. Far too often such analytic procedures are predicated on an inductive approach to analysis. Prior theorising or speculation is eschewed in favour of a close, repeated inspection of the data in the hope or expectation that patterns, regularities and themes will 'emerge' or reveal themselves. Now, that may not be the intention of those textbook authors, but that is too frequently the effect. In consequence, 'analysis' becomes divorced from fieldwork, treated as a matter of procedure or protocol. The original inspiration of, say, GT is all but obliterated.

The originators of such perspectives on 'analysis' never intended them to be exercises in purely inductive inference, nor were they intended to be restricted to the inspection of a corpus of otherwise inert 'data'. At root, they are representations of processes whereby *ideas* and *observations* are brought into dialogue. When we read, or listen to, or look at 'data', we ask ourselves what ideas can illuminate them. We bring into play existing ideas, deriving from our disciplinary knowledge, and we try to generate ideas. The ideas are brought together with each other as well as with the data. Such productive engagement is not confined to a separate period of 'analysis'. It is present in our minds when we are in the field, when we write up our field notes, when we transcribe recordings and when we write analytic memoranda. There is a repeated process of speculation and of canvassing the relevance and application of a range of ideas. Older and newer ideas feed into one another. It is not just a matter of using field-work to illustrate existing ideas, nor does it imply a falsificationist attempt to 'test' those ideas against new observations, although repeated processes of trying out our ideas should be taking place.

Such activity obviously requires close attention to the fieldwork and the information it yields. It calls for an imaginative and well-informed, detailed engagement in the field and with one's data. In the interests of such thinking, and in the spirit of Harry Wolcott, I want to advocate learning a lot from a little as opposed to learning a little from a lot. As a series of methodological exercises, therefore, the short studies that make up most of this book are based on that principle. I challenge myself to document things in detail and to reflect upon them as best I can, trying to transform brief incursions into unfamiliar settings and activities into occasions for analytic thought and methodological reflection.

The substantive themes in this book are, as I have hinted above, about technique and expertise, about embodiment, the hand and the eye, the tool and the hand. It is concerned with the ethnographic acquisition of knowledge, and of rudimentary technical competence. It is an exploration of learning, and hence of teaching, especially the embodied authority of teachers. Much of this can be glossed as 'craft' insofar as several of the things I write about are conventionally thought of as crafts, such as glassblowing or ceramics, and other activities, such as photography and life-drawing, also involve craft-like techniques.

The brief fieldwork exercises and their consequences will be described in considerably more detail in following chapters. Here I introduce them, by way of outlining the contents of the rest of this book. Initially, and quite deliberately, much of the fieldwork, and hence of the writing, is about my own efforts and attempts to learn elementary skills. So what are those 'craft' activities? It began seriously with glassblowing. I find glass artefacts very pleasing, and I already owned several pieces of modern Scandinavian glass. There is a major glass-blowing studio near our pied-a-terre in South London. Having formulated a rough intention to 'do' something with craft artists, I visited the London Glass Studio in Bermondsey. Like many such studios, it is open to visitors. There is a gallery selling pieces by the various makers at the front and at the back, the makers themselves are visible, creating blown glass vessels. At the liminal space between the gallery and the workshop, visitors are free to sit and watch the craftworkers. There is a very clear contrast between the brightly lit shelves and the finished pieces in the gallery space and the industrial air of the studio itself. I wandered into the studio and sat watching some of the craftworkers creating glass vessels. I ventured to introduce myself, and found myself talking to Peter Layton, the proprietor of the studio, a leading designer and maker of glass. I explained my general interest, and he suggested that studying the studio and his colleagues was entirely feasible. But he suggested – perhaps insisted – that I should take one of their classes as a preliminary or prerequisite to any further observation. I readily agreed, and so planned to undertake my first taste of craft learning. The studio is famous for the pioneering work of Peter Layton himself, and of the makers who work there with him (Layton 1996, 2006). I learned about embodied skills and techniques.

That was followed by a similar exercise in ceramics. I had some slight knowledge of studio pottery, and owned several pieces by well-known potters, and I was keen to extend my knowledge of the process of making. Out of the blue I contacted a potter called Chris Keenan, who has a studio in South London. He was willing to have me visit the studio, and I spent several separate days watching him throw pots, turn and glaze them, and remove fired pots from his kiln. He talked while he worked. Subsequently it became clear to me that I really ought to try to gain some hands-on experience of clay. Chris does not regularly offer classes, but I consulted him as to who I might approach. I was delighted when he offered tuition himself. And so, with his expert guidance, I learned the rudiments of throwing and turning, and made some pots which Chris then glazed and fired for me. I started to learn more about physical coordination and working with material means.

Nic Webb was working in the same cluster of studios as Chris Keenan, and Chris recommended him to me. Nic is a master craftsman in wood and clay. His work features in major exhibitions and collections. He uses a combination of traditional and experimental techniques in creating a wide variety of vessels. He also conducts one-day classes on spoon-making. He himself creates a large number of wooden spoons, in a range of sizes and made from all sorts of different woods. So together with two other learners, I took one of his one-day classes, whittling a spoon from part of a tree branch. I learned a good deal in a short time about tools and their embodied use.

I met Ellie Swinhoe at a craft fair, and was struck by the jewellery she made – bold, innovative pieces that were also eminently wearable. We talked a little, amidst the bustle of a busy fair, and I agreed to go and visit her at her studio (also her home) in Frome (Somerset), a town that has a concentration of makers and artists. I then arranged for Ellie to give me a class in silversmithing, when together we made a very simple silver ring. I later spent another day with her, this time on the slightly more ambitious project of making a silver spoon. I learned yet more about materials and materiality with her.

Not all of my learning experiences have been based on such craft-based making. Two of my exercises have involved visual activities. I took a week-long class in life-drawing, with Rachel Clark in her East London studio. Unlike my other classes, this was a group activity, with eight students, each working at their own easel. I had briefly, and very ineptly, tried life-drawing while a student at Cambridge, but this was my first real attempt, with a tutor guiding me. I made a large number of drawings in charcoal, with varying degrees of success. In the process, I learned something about observation and concentration.

I then followed this up with a course in photography, or more precisely in digital photography. As a young man, I acquired skills in film photography – developing and printing my own black-and-white images. But my recent and current photography was based on digital cameras, and printing at home on my computer and basic printer. I realised that despite my previous photographic experience, I was using even a sophisticated camera in 'auto' mode, relying on its automatic settings, and essentially using it in a 'point-and-shoot' way. Of course, the resulting pictures were mostly well exposed and focused – because modern cameras are very good at that – but the overall experience was not satisfying. Equally, I wanted to parallel the experience of life drawing with nude art photography. Therefore I engaged a London-based tutor, Ion Paciu, who runs a photography school (PhotoIon). We spent several intensive days together, as I tried to re-learn how to take photographs as opposed to lazy snapping while travelling or doing fieldwork. One of the days was spent with a professional model, in a temporary studio in rented space near Waterloo in South London. I had to re-learn how to make a photograph, and how to act like a photographer, rather than just taking pictures.

Clearly, those exercises had taxed various senses (vision, touch) and actions (tool use, posture, breathing) but none had been focused specifically on smell. In discussion with Mila Steele, my then editor at SAGE, we decided to take a perfume course together at a studio in East London, the Experimental Perfume Club. And having taken the course, the following year I did it again, this time with my colleague Dr Rhiannon Evans. It is a very concentrated course, and in some ways the most difficult to write about – not because it is problematic in itself, but because smell is such a tricky, nebulous phenomenon to capture and describe. Each of the classes was led by professional perfumer Emmanuelle Moeglin.

Before I embarked on those learning activities, and together with my colleague Dr Maggie Gregory, I followed a course of evening classes in Argentine tango. While I never attained any degree of proficiency in the dance itself, it does provide me with the opportunity to reflect on embodiment and rhythm. Tango has been the focus of a substantial body of work in anthropology, cultural studies and ethnomusicology. I do not attempt to rival any of that literature, but to use 'my' tango to illustrate some issues in embodied ethnography. Towards the end of the next chapter, I shall touch on what I learned from my efforts at learning tango.

These in outline form the substantive background to this book. I have not gone into much detail here about the exercises or my ethnographic practice. The series of activities was never conceived as a 'research' exercise proper. I did not start with any grand scheme. I followed my nose, giving in to my own curiosity. There is, therefore, no single analytic motif that motivates this work, except for a recurrent interest in skill, knowledge, craft – applied to the substantive topics I describe, and to the conduct of ethnographic work itself. In the next chapter, I introduce some of the key ideas that inform this work, and some of the key studies that contribute to that understanding. Then I shall consider the very many contributions made by sociologists and anthropologists to a collective understanding of knowledge, skill and craft knowledge. I shall elaborate on the commitment of ethnographers to the acquisition and explication of everyday and specialist knowledge. In doing so, I shall also reflect on our collective need to retain our focus on the phenomena of work, materials and methods. I shall re-visit some of the complaints levelled against studies that 'lose' or overlook those phenomena. I shall be arguing that even recent calls for research based on 'sensory' ethnography can too readily overlook aspects of sensory experience.

I should, before proceeding any further, make it clear that these various activities I have undertaken – with the exception of the opera masterclass – were not undertaken with the overarching plan of anything approaching a multi-site ethnography. They were each pursued for two purposes: as personal explorations and as methodological exercises. Equally, my work does not rival major studies in which an anthropologist or sociologist has become apprenticed to a single craft or aesthetic discipline: some of those studies I shall refer to in the following chapter. Being a committed ethnographer, I did keep detailed field notes in the course of those exercises. After hours 'in the field' in the studio, I would devote more hours writing or dictating detailed observations and reflections. All of those texts, lightly edited, have been shared with the people who had attempted to instruct and help me. They have also seen relevant chapters from this book. It will be seen that I refer to them by name, and have not substituted pseudonyms. My main reasons are practical and interpersonal. It becomes meaningless if one has spent time with leading, well-known practitioners, each with her or his distinctive style and body of work – and then pretend that they are just un-named and unacknowledged 'tutors'. Each has seen and had the opportunity to comment on my notes and thoughts on our time and work together. Where there were other 'students', I have refrained from making reference to them individually. Likewise, I have given the photographic model referred to in Chapter 7 a pseudonym, not least because she and her images would be readily traceable through social media such as Instagram.

I shall expand on this towards the end of the book, but here I make clear that I do not regard the following chapters as being autoethnography. I am not interested in practising autoethnography in the sense that 'it's all about me'. I do not write about these things in order to explore – however 'sensitively' – my personal, emotional responses to the fieldwork, except insofar as they might illuminate the real topics of my research and writing. They are concerned with: materials, tools and techniques; embodied skill and the senses; surfaces and appearances; vision and observation. These are enduring and pervasive issues in ethnographic research in many settings, and they go well beyond the personal and the emotive. So, not an exercise in autoethnography, this *is* more akin to a series of exercises in practical phenomenology (see Schröer Hinnenkamp, Kreher and Poferl

2012). As I have already mentioned, there is always a danger, even in detailed ethnographic research, of 'losing the phenomenon'. In brief, social scientists all too often study something in order to argue about *something else*. Those 'other' topics are often the stock-in-trade of sociological interest – class, gender or race – and the study of practical activities becomes the means to study social networks, influence, power or privilege. Hence the study of 'craft' skills can become a stalking-horse for critiques of neo-liberalism, globalisation or the substitution of robotics for human workers. All of those 'big picture' issues are of potential significance, self-evidently. But it is too easy to lose sight of what 'work' actually consists of in pursuit of analyses of the means of production and critiques of neoliberalism. Here, as will become apparent in the chapters that follow, I remain focused on the concrete phenomena of craft skill and its embodied practices.

To return to a comment made at the very beginning of this chapter, I am thoroughly committed to ethnographic research *as* a practical activity and *on* practical activity. I am committed to ethnographic studies of what people actually *do*. Far too many studies that pass for ethnographic, or more broadly as 'qualitative', seem to be dependent on talk, mostly derived from interviews. Now, I am not making an over-simplified distinction between talk and actions. Talk is clearly composed of spoken actions, speech-acts and performances that accomplish work in themselves. But my complaint here is a more elementary one. We justify ethnographic research in terms of the value of participant observation, only to find that many published accounts report little or nothing of observed events – let alone of participation – but rely on informants' accounts. Interview extracts seem to be much more easy to deploy by way of illustration than carefully assembled and thoroughly explored accounts of what people actually do. 'Everyday life' thus gets emptied of the practical activities of everyday actions, of things and of work. It goes without saying, I hope, that I have not observed and participated in grim silence, eschewing all forms and occasions for talk. One can hardly spend hours or days with a teacher, trying to learn new skills, without the exchange of talk. But ultimately I find interview materials poor in comparison with direct observation and participation. I also find it more fruitful, when possible, to talk with craft makers while they are working, so that they can *show* me what they are talking about and can *tell* me what they are doing. Of course, that was not a possible strategy in, say, the perfume lab or in the life-drawing studio, where a group of us were learning and working, rather than my observing and talking to a solitary maker. The critique of interviewing has been explored on multiple occasions, and I do not rehearse those debates here. They are well known, see Atkinson and Silverman (1997); Hammersley (2017); Silverman (2017); Whitaker and Atkinson (2019a, b).

As I have intimated, those activities I undertook as a participant were primarily methodological in character and intent. I have, therefore, set myself some challenges. Given that I am committed to attention to the phenomena, and to documenting 'thick participation', one of the major challenges is just how to write about those matters. A thorough account of materials, surfaces, scents and so on places particular demands on the ethnographer-as-author. It is by no means straightforward to describe and to convey those elusive phenomena that are, in part at least, dependent on one's senses. It is a more elusive goal than just reporting extracts of talk, or even of reporting the actions of others. It does depend on a considerable effort of reconstruction that owes more than a little to introspection and imaginative recall. It is in that sense, therefore, that certain aspects of this book might look autoethnographic. But I repeat that my emphasis here is on technique and learning. My personal feelings are relevant up to a point, but only insofar as they contribute to the bigger analytic picture.

2

Ethnographic Knowing

Ethnographic fascination

In this chapter, I explore some of the issues involved in the ethnographic acquisition of knowledge and competence. In particular, I examine processes whereby fieldwork leads to specialised knowledge or practical competence in a given activity. It is about how the ethnographer becomes adequately proficient in the tasks and activities of a given social domain – such as an occupation or profession, a performance art or, in my case, in 'craft' work. It therefore explores how the ethnographer might move between those positions, so beloved of methods textbooks, of 'insider' and 'outsider'. Such distinctions can have pedagogic uses, but in the complex realities of ethnographic fieldwork, they are over-simplified at best. In some cases, the ethnographer certainly aspires to 'insider' expertise, at least to an elementary degree. Indeed, there are many settings where it is almost impossible *not* to gain some degree of insider knowledge, and where it would be impossible to understand that setting without doing so. It therefore bears on the recurrent dilemmas of going native.

'Going native' has been a recurrent trope in the history of ethnographic work, especially in anthropology. Its negative connotations reflect anxieties and preoccupations that haunted anthropology – and European culture – from its origins. Indeed they derive precisely *from* those origins. Encounters, direct or at a distance, with the strangers of elsewhere engendered a variety of conflicting responses. The exotic and the primitive could instil fascination and attraction. Literary and artistic circles could embrace 'native' or 'primitive' forms and motifs. Successive expeditions to Africa furnished Parisian artists with images of Negritude that could provide models for modernist painting and sculpture. Likewise, primitive cultures could be brought into aesthetic alignment with modernist movements like surrealism. Modernist encounters with exotic otherness extended to the discovery of pre-classical Aegean civilisations.

The forms of Cycladic and Minoan graphic and plastic art furnished models of a stark simplicity and formal elegance that contributed to modernist aesthetics (Gere 2009). The fact that they preceded the familiar classical forms associated with academic art – contributed to the intrigue, and a sense of even greater distance from twentieth-century conversations. There could be a prurient preoccupation with 'the other' – a simultaneous attraction and repulsion, instanced in a male, hegemonic gaze and an optic fascination with exotic, alien and highly sexualised 'primitive' female bodies. Specimens such as 'The Hottentot Venus' were inspected for their different, native and primitive anatomy (Crais and Scully 2010; Qureshi 2004). So going native, in its colonialist sense, could express a positive pull towards the primitive. It was found in practice in many geographical and cultural milieux. Orientalist preoccupations could lead European explorers to adopt Arab or Turkish cultural conventions. If not 'primitive', such cultural affiliations endorsed the exotic nature of the 'native' and the temptations of going native.

To go native is to abandon that social and cultural distance that separates the ethnographer from those 'others' who are the subjects of interest. Insofar as the idea persists – though not necessarily known by the same terms – it refers to the elision of that experiential and intellectual distance. The ethnographer who goes native loses her or his intellectual autonomy and mobility. Rather than maintaining distance, her or his immersion in the field becomes both unconditional and barely reversible. It is a process of *becoming* that renders impossible critical reflection. Cultural forms and social relations become habitual and taken for granted: the absolute antithesis of their becoming topics of deliberative analysis. So the 'danger' of going native for most current ethnographers is not based on the moral contamination of over-identification with the 'others'. Rather, it resides in the consequent blunting of any analytic edge. When familiarity tips over into over-familiarity, then the would-be ethnographer's analytic gaze can lose its focus. Familiarity becomes an encompassing hindrance (Delamont and Atkinson 2021). There are, of course, ethnographers who work among 'their own', who *are* natives in that sense. Their analytic challenge is equivalent, but their starting point is diametrically opposed. They *start* their ethnographic exercise with taken-for-granted competence. As I noted in the previous chapter, one original meaning of 'autoethnography' was the study of a social world of which one was already a member. So the would-be ethnographer is possessed of socialised competence, but may find it hard (if not impossible) to step back from taken-for-granted realities in order to interrogate them.

Now going native and/or being native are not my approach in this book, nor indeed in my other publications. But that does *not* imply that I, or any other field researcher, should remain aloof from everyday competence, knowledge or skills. Equally, we should not seek to immerse ourselves so thoroughly and for such extended periods that we lose our identity *as* ethnographers or lose sight of why we undertake ethnographic fieldwork. What we need to cultivate is an iterative process of fieldwork and critical, analytic reflection. Equally I realise that 'going native', troubling through that vocabulary may be, resonates with some of the preoccupations expressed in this book. It captures the possibility, at least, of such an intensely focused preoccupation with the chosen social world that it becomes the dominant way of seeing, thinking and acting that it overcomes the scholar's first allegiance to her or his research commitments. It is a shift of allegiance born of fascination. It is a form of cultural conversation. It reverses the kind of appropriation that is an inherent danger in all fieldwork. Rather than the ethnographer's return, bearing the concrete and symbolic trophies of her success, she is in turn captured by the host culture. 'Going native' recalls the Latin tag, that Rome, having made Greece captive, was in turn captivated by Greece. It reminds us that fieldwork in virtually any setting is *absorbing* and even *seductive*. One may, therefore, be fascinated and learn from that fascination without complete surrender. In my incursions into the fields of craft production and performance, therefore, I commit myself to learning as much as possible without succumbing to the 'native's' social world. An aliquot of fieldwork provides, temporarily, wholehearted commitment without complete and unconditional loss of identity and purpose.

Ethnographic knowledge

Apprenticeship and the acquisition of practical knowledge have a certain currency in anthropological and sociological work (Martin 2021, p. 17ff.). Studies of apprenticeship have focused particularly on performance, art and craft activities. But Downey et al. (2015) conclude that:

> Enculturation happens to all fieldworkers. Apprenticeship processes are not unique to ethnography in performance traditions, since … some kind of cultural apprenticeship occurs in all field sites. Processes of culture-making are, however, given a privileged stance in learning environments like the ones we write about, where individuals' progress is actively analysed, explained and guided by teachers as students move toward the shared goal of cultural competency. The particularities of apprenticeship as method highlight shared problems for all ethnographers, bringing into focus the limits and

opportunities generated by a method that requires balancing immersion and participation with systematic observation. (pp. 196–197)

Those authors were writing specifically about sports and similar physical
activities, and their specific emphasis is – as in my own exercises – on
embodied action. But they are right, in that all ethnographic fieldwork
inevitably results in the researcher's acquisition of specialised, sometimes
esoteric, knowledge and skills. As we shall see, it can also involve the
acquisition of practical competence, at least at some elementary level, on
the part of the ethnographer. And when the fieldwork includes some
element of full participation, then such learning is an anticipated outcome
of the ethnographic encounter(s).

Quite apart from the specific studies I shall be developing in the chapters
that follow, there are some significant methodological issues touched on in
this context. They include the generic question: How much local or specialised knowledge does the ethnographer need to aspire to and to acquire?
One extreme version of this resides in the notion of *unique adequacy*,
articulated by a number of ethnomethodologists. It exists in weaker and
stronger versions. Garfinkel and Wieder (1992, p. 182) argued that the
researcher must become 'vulgarly competent' in order to recognise and
describe the production of social action and orderly conduct in any given
social setting. Vulgar competence could cover a broad spectrum of
understanding. It clearly falls short of expert knowledge, implying a level
of competence sufficient to allow the ethnographer to make sense of
the specifics of local activities. It certainly implies an engagement with the
particulars and the content of organised action. It thus goes beyond the
kind of interactionist study of socialisation that is conducted at such a level
of generality (negotiation, perspectives, situated learning) that it falls short
of accounting for the specific contents of work, education or indeed of
everyday collective activity. I take it that, in terms set out by Schütz, vulgar
competence goes beyond the knowledge of the 'well-informed citizen', but
falls short of that of the scientist or expert (Schütz 1976). In phenomenological terms, it is a form of knowledge that allows practical expertise
and performance. The sociologist of medicine might, therefore, become
vulgarly competent in recognising specific traits, syndromes, signs and
symptoms, without acquiring the underlying knowledge of anatomy,
physiology or clinical pathology; the criminologist may need to gain
knowledge of the law in certain specialisms, without becoming a legal
expert; the sociologist of music does not necessarily need to be a skilled
instrumentalist or singer.

In much ethnographic research, even in classic studies, the specific
competence of the participants is barely visible, if at all. Readers gain
little or no understanding of just what practitioners do, and what

therefore makes their social world, occupation or vocation distinctive and special. I take just one specific example here that relates back to my own earlier work. In a classic interactionist study of medical education, Becker et al. (1961) published a major monograph on the medical school as a social institution in which the (nearly all male) students were faced by almost insurmountable demands. It is a learning environment in which students are expected to assimilate vast amounts of factual information, as well as learning how to put it to use. In response, as Becker and his colleagues explain, the students developed and devised collective coping strategies, similar to those described in studies of shop-floor workers, in trying to establish their own levels and directions of effort. As a contribution to the study of student culture, the monograph was an important achievement, and it did much to illuminate productive ideas such as 'the hidden curriculum'. But little attention was really paid to the 'what' of medical knowledge and skill that formed the subject matter and the everyday preoccupations of medical students and their instructors. *Boys in White*, for all its length and scope, does little to teach us what versions of medical knowledge are required, how such knowledge is translated into pedagogy and practice or just what doctoring skills those students acquired (or failed to). It became my intention in my own monograph to go at least some way towards rectifying that absence (Atkinson 1981).

So, to return to my main argument, the weaker version of the adequacy requirement is readily endorsed. It should be hard to envisage an ethnography of a specialised setting that is not at least enhanced by the analyst's basic grasp (vulgar competence) of the local systems of knowledge and practice. On the other hand, the stronger version seems harder to sustain. There have been very few studies that really approach that strong version, which stipulates that the researcher and the practitioner should have levels of expertise equivalent to those of practitioners themselves. As Pollner and Emerson (2007, p. 131) put it: 'Extreme immersion on the one hand and hyper-reflexivity on the other obliterate the very distinction between researcher and member, observer and observed, enquiry and object'. The classic example of work in that vein is Livingston's monograph on the work of mathematics (Livingston 1986). Livingston spent years in the acquisition of graduate-level mathematics in order to study the practical work involved in proving a mathematical theorem. Mathematics itself is, of course, sometimes chosen as the hardest case in order to demonstrate 'social' aspects of science and knowledge, and Livingston's exercise is egregious, in that he tackled some of the most esoteric expertise. (His use of mathematics has not been without criticism: it has been disputed whether what he describes is actually a proof, but that is not especially germane here.) Livingston's work does, however, exemplify two major limitations to the stronger version of the unique adequacy requirement. The first limitation is the extent to which it restricts the researcher to competence in just one set of skills. It takes no account of a division of labour and a distribution of competence within a given social world. It is one thing to do mathematics as a single practitioner – although maths can also be worked on collectively at the chalk board. But one cannot study an opera company just by following a lengthy period of training as a singer or a musician, or as a lighting designer or costume maker, or a stage-crew member, or an artisan in the props department. One cannot understand the music department of that opera company without some regard for the complementary but different work of the conductor, the répétiteur or the orchestra member. And so on. In other words, the strong version of unique adequacy requires a focus on just *one* kind of activity, ideally undertaken in relative isolation. In some fields of sociological research, there is indeed a tendency to 'see' just the single specialist, and to take insufficient interest in the local division of labour. For instance, it seems that too many studies of scientists focus solely on the individual 'top' scientists, rather than members of their laboratory teams – technicians, research assistants, postdoctoral fellows or post-graduate students. But to acquire the 'right' level and kind of knowledge for each of those categories would be all but impossible. Hence the 'strongest' version of unique adequacy is impossible to implement in any meaningfully ethnographic sense.

Since apprenticeship in just one set of skilful practices demands full-time, long-term immersion, the would-be ethnographer can really only study *one* science, or craft, a time. Her or his social and geographical mobility within and across social worlds is severely limited. So the strong requirement for unique adequacy is the antithesis of the ethnographer's fear of going native. For a researcher like Livingston, the would-be field researcher must virtually disappear from research in order to gain adequate expertise. For all but a tiny minority, such a strategy would be practically impossible and methodologically erroneous. Even Pollner and Emerson are forced to conclude that this is not a sustainable research practice. Followed by his studies of puzzles, origami and similar activities (Livingston 2008), Livingston's remains a niche approach, although – as we shall see – it has affinities with many other ethnographic projects that are based on processes of *learning*. But any implication that expertise is a prerequisite for successful research on specialised knowledge is a dead end for any practical fieldwork. Indeed, the enculturated and fully competent ethnographer would be in a position equivalent to that of the 'insider' practitioner-researcher.

The insider researcher, who tries to work on her or his own social world – often their workplace or professional practice – faces recurrent problems of familiarity and strangeness. Because she or he is fully enculturated, it can be extremely difficult to establish any analytic perspective. The problem is that the practitioner routinely finds it hard to 'see' phenomena that she or he routinely takes for granted. It can be proverbially hard for the everyday actor or skilled practitioner to make what is done into a topic of explicit attention. When it is focused on, it is often done so in a judgemental spirit, through the evaluation of others' performance against acquired norms. Again an *analytic* approach can be hard to achieve and sustain.

The answer is, therefore, neither aloof distance nor the search for unrealisable competence. Rather, my approach, based as it is on short-term incursions into different 'fields', attempts to alternate immersion and distance, moving between observation and participation, paying close attention to the practicalities of work and the acquisition of modest, even minimal, competence. Basic competence, therefore, is my aim in these practical exercises. It is not, and never was, a matter of 'becoming'. There is no intention here to develop into even an adequate amateur or hobbyist. As we shall see, several ethnographers have followed that route, by pursuing the course of an apprenticeship, and over an extended period of time, they acquire a thorough grounding in the craft or science, and can achieve a decent level of practice.

Pre-textual ethnography

Part of the rationale for my approach, based on an aliquot of fieldwork, is to explore the nature of what has recently been called pre-textual fieldwork. Inevitably, of course, ethnography generates texts – field notes and transcripts among them – and these texts are the building blocks of further texts in the form of journal papers and monographs. But the thrust of pre-textual work derives from an engagement with materials and the senses. Pre-textual ethnography is, for its advocates, a reaction against the kind of analysis derived from Geertz, that treats culture as a kind of text, or assemblage of texts, that present themselves for interpretation. Ethnography in that vein is a kind of 'reading', or hermeneutic exercise. As Rakowski and Patzer (2018) summarise it:

> The challenge is then to build a kind of sensual ethnography and ethnographic language, even if we are equipped with the scientific tradition of a disembodied mode of observation. (p. 9)

They argue against any view that embodied activity is in any way 'merely' habitual or automatic. In pursuit of such a pre-textual ethnography, they invoke Samudra (2008) on 'thick participation', by which is meant 'cultural knowledge recorded first in the anthropologist's body and only later externalised as visual or textual data for purposes of analysis' (p. 667). I am not quite convinced that experience incarnate is in any sense *prior* to those other forms, as there should always be a dialogue between the modalities of experiencing and understanding. But the contrast between thick participation and thick description is an encouraging one, placing the emphasis on practical activity and engagement with the world (physical and cultural) rather than on the more distanced, cerebral connotations of description and interpretation. As we shall see, my emphasis through most of this book is on embodied learning and doing, on thick participation, and to that extent perhaps is in part pre-textual ethnography.

In much the same vein is Dalsgård's appeal to phenomenology (2018), in pursuit of a 'radical empiricism' for ethnography (cf. Jackson 1989), and stressing the fact that phenomenological enquiry, grounded in the imaginative act of bracketing (epoché), is not a solipsistic exercise in navel-gazing but rests on interaction with the surrounding world. Certainly that is the kind of inspiration I gain from the phenomenologists – as indeed from the pragmatism of symbolic interaction – that sense of concrete engagement with one's immediate world. Research, as everyday exploration, lies in practical encounters, and social research is but an extension of ordinary learning and interaction. Indeed, I take seriously the view that ethnography resides in the methods of everyday life, grown self-conscious, in exploring everyday life itself (Atkinson 2015a). It must be kept in mind that phenomenological bracketing and the consequent estrangement of the world is not a sudden epiphany, an unforeseen tearing of the veil of common sense. It is something we have to *work* at, if only to get beyond immediate, and probably superficial, experiences of 'strangeness' or 'otherness'. One certainly cannot expect a sudden revelation of phenomenological enlightenment. In a similar vein, Hastrup (2018) uses Bachelard's (1964) use of 'muscular consciousness' to convey the dialectical relationship between active consciousness and the world we explore, while Lenk (2018) acknowledges that '...it took me almost half way through fieldwork to realise that understanding was also based on our shared bodily presence and the ability, or willingness, to quiet the mind and listen with the senses. It took some time before I was able to let things, people and knowledge to reveal themselves' (p. 191). Now, as I have just suggested, I do not think we can or should depend on things or actors 'revealing themselves', but that sense of bodily participation and sensory engagement – *thick participation* – is central to the methodological exercises reported throughout the remainder of this book.

The transformation of 'pre-textual', sensory (and sensual) ethnographic practice, and the incarnate experience it engenders, into textual forms remains a challenge, of course. Embodied and sensory experience as a basis for ethnographic understanding cannot substitute for the need for sustained *analysis*. We are not in the business of amassing 'impressions' or documenting 'experiences'. This is, as I have tried to make clear, not an exercise in solipsistic reflection, nor is it a narcissistic autoethnography (Atkinson 2006c). But the spirit of phenomenological enquiry and the strategy of thick participation mean that the observer/participant/author must use her or his own embodied presence as the starting point for an objective analysis of sensory and physical phenomena. And those are not merely about physical, sensory responses or impressions: they are about the 'phenomena' themselves – textures, surfaces, materials, appearances and so on – as they are constituted through our physical and imaginative engagements with them. As Stoller (1997) says:

> The full presence of the ethnographer's body in the field ... demands a fuller sensual awareness of the smells, tastes, sounds and textures of life among the others.... For ethnographers embodiment is more than the realization that our bodily experience gives metaphorical meaning to our experience; it is rather the realization that ...we too are consumed by the sensual world, that ethnographic things capture us through our bodies, that profound lessons are learned when sharp pains streak up our legs in the middle of the night. (p. 23)

As we shall see, sharp pains can afflict us in a photographic studio in the middle of the afternoon, or while making a wooden or a silver spoon, too.

In pursuing this line of thought, it is perhaps useful, just occasionally, to think concretely, to be overliteral in our interpretation of metaphors and other tropes, if only to see where it gets us. My theme here is knowledge, the ethnography of knowledge and our knowledge of ethnography. One such metaphor is Foucault's 'archaeology of knowledge'. Its force derives from an archaeological or geological image of stratification, stressing the discontinuity between different layers and hence attending to successive ruptures, in a view of history and understanding that is not one of continuous, steady growth or improvement. But what if we reverse the gaze and strip it all of its metaphorical status? We might rather think about 'the knowledge of archaeology'. This in turn might help turn our attention to such mundane, ordinary activities as *digging*. Hence I turn to an account by Langlands (2017), who is both an archaeologist and a practitioner of cultivation by hand. He has firsthand knowledge of digging. From his account, the knowing, experienced archaeologist knows not just how to dig but also knows what each tool and each technique will permit. S/he also knows how to look at the soil, and how to feel it, how to spot tell-tale markings and differences that the spade might reveal. The eye, the tool and the hand reveal: how to spot the subtle changes in colour and texture that indicate features (such as post-holes); the changes that mark and differentiate the levels in a trench; the difference between a natural feature and one made by human actors. As Langlands says:

> ... swinging a mattock in the service of archaeology is rather different from using it to break ground. Because care and attention are required when excavating valuable archaeological deposits, and because you're often working in confined spaces with other archaeologists, the business end of the mattock is rarely lifted above the head and swung wildly down. The technique becomes more one of a chipping away, of retaining enough control to pull out of the motion should you expose what might be an important archaeological find. Even so, it's just as laborious, and more so if you have to spend all day bent double. (p. 301)

The working craft knowledge of archaeology is obviously about far more than digging. It calls for a knowledge of stratigraphy; of pollens, land snails and tree rings; of surveying and dating technologies. But that clear and simple statement helps illuminate more general issues of skill and understanding in many specialist fields. It also reminds us that many kinds of expertise rest on the deployment of relatively simple actions that in turn inscribe the kind of competence painstakingly acquired over the course of enculturation. The skilled use of the tool, coordinated with the body and the eye, is at the heart of craft knowledge and expertise.

The pre-textual in the textual, the practical knowledge that may underpin ethnographic analysis, therefore, offers just one avenue of enquiry into our understanding of craft, and of the craft of ethnography. It does not supplant or suppress other forms of ethnographic enquiry. It is an approach that focuses our individual and collective attention on practical action. It moves us some distance away from the talk-centred style of much that passes for ethnographic research. The almost obsessive focus on the conduct of interviews, and the consequent lack of attention to practical, concrete action, needs to be balanced by the kind of work I am referring to and advocating here. Luckily there are plenty of examples to help us shape such projects. Anthropological and sociological studies of knowledge in action, and of the acquisition of skilled competence, are significant in number and for their quality. Many involve the ethnographer 'joining in' as a participant, developing some degree of proficiency and writing about that process in the form of ethnographic analysis. Such ethnographic attention to the practicalities of knowledge and its acquisition make some discussions of 'tacit knowledge' (Polanyi 1958; Collins 2010) seem jejune. Explicit verbal instructions or formulae self-evidently do not generate expected outcomes or competence, but there is nothing mysterious about practical knowledge in action. We acquire it through the simultaneous use of language, gesture, haptic sensations and other sensory comprehension. Mentors demonstrate, encourage, correct, intervene and chide. Like the operatic masterclasses we studied, any 'class' in craft is a multimodal dialogue.

Knowledge in action

Anthropology has long focused on issues of knowledge, materials and skill – though not always as central topics of enquiry. Malinowski's detailed descriptions of Trobriand cultivation (*Coral Gardens and their Magic*, 1935) are a case in point. Among the classics of anthropology is one that treats the subject matter of this book as central. Marcel Mauss (2006) made *technique* a major, guiding theme in his work. Readers of Mauss's work have long been familiar with his analysis of 'the techniques of the body', which became a *locus classicus* in the emergent anthropology and sociology of the body in the second half of the twentieth century. It continues to be an important source for an understanding of the body as a culturally shaped presence, in which the most apparently 'natural' of behaviours are culture specific. But acquaintance with that work alone would lead one to overlook that the main idea is 'technique' rather than just embodied performativity. For Mauss, the analysis of technique is an entrée into the entirety of human enculturated activity. There is, after all, little or nothing that we do that is not based on knowing what to do and knowing how to do it. Technique offers a focus on just those practical competences that make possible our more-or-less skilful actions. Technique thus links the human and the natural: technique permits us to work with and on the material world. Technique allows us to see the possibilities in materials, in wood, stone, clay, wool or leather. It links the eye of the actor with the tools at hand, the material circumstance to be dealt with and the world about her. Technique reminds us that nothing is accomplished without thorough – sometimes protracted – learning. Technique is passed down from generation to generation; from mentor to apprentice; from teacher to student. But it cannot be reduced to simple instructions and formulae. It is acquired through practice, and through embodied competence. It relates the hand to the eye, and to a knowledge of cultural forms (physical and symbolic). In some ways that I will not develop fully here, Mauss's emphasis on technique is analogous to the later concerns of ethnomethodology, as mediated through phenomenology. All three perspectives – Mauss, phenomenology, ethnomethodology – direct our attention to the particularities of practical activity, to the skills that actors deploy in achieving their ends and the acquisition of competence. They all commend close observation and scrutiny of *how* actors perform their everyday tasks as well as *what* they actually do.

In Mauss's terms, techniques are 'taught, acquired, transmitted' (Schlanger 2006, p. 18), and in his treatment of habitual bodily action, Mauss clearly prefigured Bourdieu on *habitus* as embodied competence. In 1935, he expressed his view in this way:

> These 'habits' do not just vary with individuals and their imitations; they vary especially between societies, educations, proprieties and fashions, prestige. In them we should see the techniques and work of collective and individual practical reason rather than, in the ordinary way, merely the soul and its repetitive faculties. (Mauss 1935/2006 'Text 9', p. 80)

Mauss insists on the collective nature of technique as well as its cultural specificity. Insofar as techniques can be embedded in 'tradition', it is because they are shared, taught and emulated or borrowed, not because tradition exerts some independent force in its own right. The spirit of Mauss's ethnology is to be found running through multiple texts of technique, that explore the practical accomplishments – the knowledge in action – of skilled, competent practitioners and their use of materials, tools, designs and plans. Indeed, to return to a more general point, one could argue that such analytic issues are at the heart of anthropological understanding. Fashioning encompasses not just the creation of objects (pots, baskets, canoes and so on) but also the self-making of the makers, and the establishment of social relations (through exchange, collaboration or apprenticeship). The same is true of ethnographic fashioning, whereby the researcher transmutes her or his ingredients into the serviceable artefacts that are monographs or other texts, while simultaneously fashioning herself or himself into an accomplished and time-served ethnographer, able to demonstrate 'mastery' of the craft and also able to cite 'experience' in the field as a source of personal and sapiential authority.

There is, therefore, a direct parallel between the social practices of apprenticeship and the making of ethnography. Downey et al. (2015) have made the point that there is an important homology between craft apprenticeships and the ethnographer's work of cultural learning.

Equally, Esther Goody (1989) suggested that apprenticeship itself is an ideal subject for anthropological investigation, as the ethnographer can learn esoteric knowledge at the same time as studying processes of enculturation itself (as in my own study of medical education). Lave and Wenger's notion of legitimate peripheral participation (Lave and Wenger 1991) captures aspects of ethnographic research and of apprenticeship at the same time (cf. Lave 2011). Wellin and Fine (2001) draw explicit comparisons between the ethnographic study of work (as in the Chicago School tradition) and the work of ethnographic research. They also note some distinctive characteristics of ethnographic socialisation, that sets it somewhat apart from much other graduate socialisation, as well as its more generic features:

> For ethnographers, socialization is embedded in a process of academic apprenticeship which, though intimate and subject to negotiation, is also regulated by evaluations and dependence on mentors. Thus, for ethnographic researchers the learning of the craft is (1) idiosyncratic across aspirants; (2) dependent on immersion in 'the field' at a distance from schools and mentors; and (3) equated symbolically with competence and occupational membership. (p. 327)

The emphasis on fieldwork apprenticeship in ethnography, with a stress on personal competence, suggests a close parallel with craft socialisation more generally. I do acknowledge, however, that each new field project can feel like a new socialisation: 'experience' is no guarantee of smooth performance. In that sense, ethnographic apprenticeship is never complete, and is – like the conduct of ethnography itself – an iterative or cyclical process.

I take it that this is also the spirit of some of Ingold's suggestion that the anthropologist's task is 'learning to learn' (Ingold 2013, p. 2). But although Ingold focuses on materiality and the practicalities of 'making', his accounts of several practices of making are sometimes perfunctory, and even his accounts of personal, firsthand experience are quite limited in scope, detail or depth. He does, however, have some fruitful observations about making in general. Although Ingold makes no reference to phenomenological investigation, his overall perspective has much in common with it. For instance, he observes that: '...the process of making is not so much an *assembly* as a *procession*, not building *up* from discrete parts into a hierarchically organised totality but a carrying *on* – a passage along a path in which every step grows from the one before and into the one following, on an itinerary that always overshoots its destinations' (p. 45, emphases in original).

In a similar vein, Ingold suggests that craftmaking is not a simple transition from an idealised plan or image – a 'design' – but an emergent process that involves repeated interactions between the maker, materials, tools and circumstances that may not be perfectly foreseen. In pursuing that idea, I argue that, rather than thinking in terms of 'design' in craftwork, it is more fruitful to think in terms of *precedents*. No maker embarks on the creation of an object with an empty mind: size, shape and constituent material must be foreshadowed. So one must 'have in mind' the *kind of* object to be made. But that must be accomplished through an iterative series of engagements that depend upon practical decisions, familiarity with tools and materials and the ability to respond to contingent events. The emergent nature of much craftwork, where each piece is conceptualised and executed as a 'one-off', separates craftwork from industrialised factory manufacture (Sennett 2008). Rather than working with a precise blueprint, the craftmaker relies on a sense of her or his materials, of style and of models and precedents. That does not mean that craftmakers cannot reproduce their own work: the potter can create a set of matching mugs or cups, and the silversmith can make a matching pair of earrings. But that is different from making on an industrial scale and pattern of work. The ethnographer cannot plan in advance precisely how her or his project will be shaped, and must be responsive to circumstances. Ethnographers have to 'find a way' to conduct their work and how to shape their materials into texts and other artefacts. The carver in wood or stone must often respond to the qualities of the material. If wood splits unexpectedly, then the craftworker can adapt to new circumstances and re-model the object. Workers in stone, wood and other materials can talk of 'finding' the form that is 'in' the block, rather than simply imposing their idea on it. Such craft practices differ quite starkly from copying or reproducing works (cf. Jordan and Weston 2003; Wong 2014). They are much more akin to the skills of the musician who can improvise, given a chord sequence or a melody (Faulkner and Becker 2009).

This is among the rationales for thick participation. The stochastic progressions that lead to the making of an artefact do not reduce themselves to formulae. For even when formulae exist, in the shape of 'instructions', it is well known that following instructions (such as those that accompany flat-packed self-assembly furniture) is by no means straightforward. Indeed, it can prove highly problematic, not to say frustrating. One has to try to 'make sense' of instructions, and for craftwork – which relies on precedent rather than instructions – one needs experience and habituated embodied skills (Garfinkel 2002; Pollner 2012). A classic description of the uncertain outcome of attempting to follow instructions, and hence the necessary reliance on social and tacit knowledge, is Collins's (1985) account of the process of building a laser. Tacit knowledge is clearly significant in the entire work of making and replicating, of translating apparently explicit instructions into workable methods: for a relevant account of a bread-making machine, see Ribeiro and Collins (2007). While written or oral instructions inform practice, they rarely determine successful learning outcomes, and novices find themselves interpreting the appearances of the desired outcome in order to make sense of the instructions. So the outcomes guide the use of instructions, rather than the reverse (See Nishizaka 2020 on the organisation of instructions).

Tacit knowledge is often embodied, carnal knowledge, and thick participation allows the ethnographer to enter into the physical, sensory world of working and making (O'Connor 2005, 2007a). Physical engagement with embodied competence and skill is a major resource for the ethnographer of learning (Marchand 2008, 2010). Embodied learning is not confined to the practical crafts, but is a fundamental feature of much pedagogy (Evans et al. 2009), although studies of pedagogy have, perhaps, too often been disembodied, focused primarily on spoken interaction. Wacquant (2004, 2005), by contrast, uses his own apprenticeship in boxing to exemplify carnal learning. Whether or not one is committed to complete participation, attention to embodied skill is always of potential significance: the subject matter can be dance (Aalten 2007), martial arts (Downey 2005) or any practical activity.

Studies of knowledge in action and its acquisition take multiple forms, but here I want to single out some studies that depend on the ethnographer/author participating and acquiring the relevant competence. Among the most prominent is David Sudnow's *Ways of the Hand* (1978), in which he details his practice in learning jazz piano. It is an outstanding exercise in phenomenology, and Sudnow applies an unusually detailed and sustained account of his own learning: how he learned to place his hands and fingers without consciously searching for the keys, and how he came to be able to estimate distances he had to reach in order to find keys and play chords accurately. In a modern classic of anthropology, Marchand (2001a) worked with minaret builders in Yemen. His account goes well beyond the basics of building, as he locates the architecture within a broader cosmology: the significance of verticality for power and piety. Likewise, he relates the phases of apprenticeship to parallel stages of Islamic spiritual enlightenment:

> ... *Islam*, or submission emphasises the embodiment of disciplined religious practice; the stage of *imam* is characterised by the cultivation of a spiritual faith and the accompanying understanding of one's ritualised practices; and *ihsan* denotes the paramount level at

which one's intentionality is fully absorbed in, and guided by, spiritual faith and understanding. These are compared with the bodily discipline inculcated in the labourer, the understanding acquired by the apprentice, and the intentionality which pervades the thoughts and action of the Master Builder and which qualifies his expert status. (p. 23, emphases in original)

Marchand describes his own practical work on a minaret, cutting bricks to shape them and naming the resulting effects created from differently shaped bricks, for instance. Comparing his participation in Yemen building and his experience of carpentry in Quebec, Marchand concludes:

For both groups, the appropriation of trade skills and expertise was achieved predominantly through observing and mimicking. This included observation of varying proportions of either the physical performance of the mentor or the object produced as final product; and the mimicry involved in repeating exercises (or practices) in order to achieve the most effective and economic (*i.e.* skilled) performance. (p. 167)

Observation and mimicry characterise the learning of the apprentice, and of the participant observer (cf. Marchand 2008). Neither Marchand nor I aspired to the position and skill of the master craftsman. But we both used our embodied participation to acquire a phenomenological grasp of practical craftwork. Because it is largely tacit, such learning does not translate readily into explicit instructions. For the same reason, writing about the processes of acquisition is always a challenge.

Marchand's study of building is just one among many anthropological and sociological studies of craft knowledge, and I shall be making more extended reference to many of them as the rest of this book unfolds. For now, I make summary reference to many of the key works. In a manner analogous to Marchand's, Haase (1998) describes his experience of being an apprentice potter in Japan. His account follows a path familiar to students of Japanese craft and discipline: he spent months repeating one basic shape of a small pot, repeatedly failing to satisfy the expectations of his teacher (*sensei*): pots judged inadequate were smashed. Since Japanese pottery can include the making of a very restricted number of forms – such as tea bowls – the repetition of basic types is a fundamental aspect of craft discipline. The craft skills of laboratory science can also mean students running experiments until they 'work' (Delamont et al. 2000). The kind of elementary learning reported in this book is nowhere near as intense as those characteristic of authentic apprenticeship, although some degree of repetition is involved in introductory lessons. Indeed, repetition will feature in several of the activities I report in later chapters.

Martin's account of working in a wooden-boat shop is instructive in examining craftworkers' tacit knowledge of materials, tools and working methods, in what they call 'the feel', grounded in a community of practice (Martin 2021). He concludes:

> Regarding how 'the feel' is experienced, my findings illustrate the boat-builders' ability to 'perceive as', or to recognize a depth of meaning in objects that is invisible to the uninitiated. In the first cases I recorded, seeing, feeling, and hearing 'as' simply meant identifying objects in terms of the processes in which they are used; for example, a paint scraper as a paint scraper. As my fieldwork progressed, however, I realized that growing familiarity with these processes led objects to transform in more radical ways, splitting apart or combining in perception as the work at hand demanded. In the moments in which I felt most comfortable with tools and materials, I found that my sense of them as discrete objects faded almost entirely, their relational interdependence within the work filling my attention instead of its individual components. (pp. 239–240)

While my own brief incursions into various studios did not equip me to become so adept, they certainly furnished that sense of work 'filling my attention', and it is a theme to which I shall return.

I acknowledge the fact that some scholars have committed themselves to prolonged apprenticeship in one craft – just as Marchand and Martin did – in the interests of ethnographic research. Most pertinently for me, O'Connor has gained practitioner competence in glass-blowing that far surpasses mine, and she is able to comment on the craft more widely and more deeply than I can. I, on the other hand, can develop a constant comparison across a much wider range of sites, while developing my argument on the basis of an 'aliquot' of fieldwork. But even if we do not, as Marchand or Haase describe, 'submit' ourselves to the extreme discipline of the traditional craft apprenticeship, our collective commitment to thick participation means that we have to surrender to the actuality of learning and practising. Fully participant observation is particularly demanding, calling for almost complete concentration on the task in hand, followed by an almost obsessive attention to documenting practices, sensations, understandings, materials, tools and outcomes. We have to become observers not just of others but, most intensively, of ourselves as well.

These exercises reflect the recurrent, abiding preoccupations of the social sciences, and of ethnography in particular. We have for decades been concerned with documenting the particularities of social knowledge. Recent calls for 'Indigenous Research' could readily create the impression that local or indigenous knowledge has historically been marginalised, neglected or devalued. While Indigenous researchers were for many years barely visible, indigenous knowledge was undoubtedly central to the ethnographic project. Consider, for instance, Gladwin's remarkable account of navigation among Pacific islanders (Gladwin 1970). The ability to sail open seas between islands that are below the horizon, without the navigation aids and charts that a modern 'Western' sailor would use, furnishes a prime example of studying the practical, local knowledge that makes it at all possible. Gladwin's emphasis is on the efficacy of such practical competence, in a way that makes that work of anthropology an early inspiration and influence for ethnomethodology. Ethnographic attention to mundane activities and practical skills means that *local* knowledge is foregrounded in a wide variety of social settings.

There are numerous studies of crafts, artisans and skilful performances. Among the most significant are: Paxson (2013) on artisan cheese making; Terrio (2000) on chocolatiers; Dudley (2014) on guitar-making; and Jones (2011) on the embodied skills of conjuring. I shall have an occasion to refer to some of those studies later in the book, as I shall return to the sustained study of glass-blowing by O'Connor. Other ethnographers who have apprenticed themselves include Chernoff (1979) who did so in order to learn the techniques of African drumming, while the learning of physical artistry includes a phenomenological account of archery by Brosziewski and Maeder (2010). These and similar accounts detail the embodiment of technique, and the acquisition of esoteric skills. All of these, and others like them, repeatedly demonstrate the artful and delicate interplay of explicit instruction and the acquisition of tacit knowledge. It might be thought that my studies of embodied competence might lean on Bourdieu's notion of *habitus* (Bourdieu 1977), denoting as it does 'dispositions' that generate culturally organised 'practices'. I do not do so here in this book, however. I find the idea and its uses, by Bourdieu and his followers, to be unhelpfully circular. It tells us that actors behave in a certain way because they have acquired a distinctive habitus. It is yet another way in which the 'over-socialised actor' is smuggled back into a sociology that claims to include actors and agency (Wrong 1961). Equally, in exploring some elements of learning and acculturation, I am not here celebrating the 'under-socialised' conception of actors (Shilling 1997). My point is simply that notions like 'habitus' can too easily short-circuit analysis, granting insufficient attention to details of technique, and failing to acknowledge degrees of acquired skill or competence.

While studies of embodiment takes us away from 'craft', we need to pay close attention to accounts of physical competence and its acquisition. Davis (2015) is but one among several who have developed a personal passion for learning and dancing tango (see also Savigliano 1995). Dance and sport provide ample opportunities for the study of embodied socialisation. For examples, see the collection of essays on martial arts, edited by García and Spencer (2013), and Downey (2005) on the Brazilian fight-dance game of *capoeira*. Delamont et al. (2017) also focus on *capoeira* in a three-way collaboration: Delamont as observer, Stephens as participant and Campos as instructor. Those and equivalent studies repeatedly demonstrate the embodied dialogue between the instructor and the novice(s): instructions must be translated into physical acts that are in turn retained as tacit actions. Novices and expert practitioners alike acquire what is often called *muscle* memory through repeated actions that become habitual. For the novice dancer or sports participant, technical moves (such as step sequences, or attacks) are objects of conscious attention. For the 'expert' practitioner, they become taken-for-granted actions – until they become learners once more (in masterclasses, for instance) when they must perform a kind of phenomenological reduction by turning habitual actions back into objects of conscious inspection and reflection (Atkinson 2013a, b).

It is important to emphasise that 'craft' work is by no means confined to activities normally associated with artisanal skill or experience. In everyday terms, the practice of 'science' – rigorous, impersonal, precise – might seem to contrast with the practical, improvisatory practice of craft. In practice, however, the sciences are thoroughly dependent on craftwork. This current work is, in a way, a continuation of earlier work I collaborated on in the past: we conducted a study of the UK Stem Cell Bank. Neil Stephens conducted the fieldwork there (Stephens et al. 2011; Stephens and Lewis 2017). Cells need to be curated, and that depends on the experience of laboratory technicians. Even in a carefully controlled environment, with multiple protocols to regulate procedures, some technicians have 'green fingers' when it comes to growing cells (Stephens et al. 2011). In the same vein, Meskus (2018) describes the role of craftwork in the laboratory, in the study of induced pluripotent stem cells. She notes:

> Numerous protocols for crafting iPS cell lines exist, but ... the disciplined and simplified world of formal guidelines seldom corresponds to the experiences of doing the stuff in the adjusted worlds of the laboratory. Much local trying, testing, and experimenting-experiencing with the living material and its substantive demands have to be conducted in order to get the cell lines growing nicely (p. 138).

The craftwork of managing 'living material' in laboratory science is repeated when it comes to the use of animal models. Animals such as mice and rats are ubiquitous in biomedical laboratories for good reasons, not least because mice can be manipulated genetically in ways that mimic human traits, while rats are conveniently used to model behavioural characteristics. The successful management of such animal models is heavily dependent on the practical expertise of animal-house technicians and scientists (Lewis et al. 2013). All practical science depends on the equivalent of artisanal craft skill (Charlesworth 1989). In the absence of personalised craftwork, there is no objective scientific knowledge. The de-contextual knowledge of scientific research rests heavily on the context-dependent knowledge of experienced practitioners (Traweek 1988).

There is nothing romantic in my interest in craft. I do not idealise the 'craftsman', and I do not endow craft practices with special values. I am especially resistant to the attribution of distinctive values to craft. Craftwork is not just about the intrinsic value of the work itself and the quality of its conduct, and it does not simply stand in stark contrast to economically driven production. It is thoroughly practical in all senses. In any event, in the course of this book, I shall not be concerned with the individual motives of the craftworkers I encountered, rather than the nature of learning, of technique and the practical engagement with tools and materials. At the same time, I repeat, these exercises are about the conduct of ethnographic enquiry and writing. There is a homology between the subject matter and the methods used to study it.

Dancing into the field: tango

While it requires less staying power than long-term ethnography, focused ethnography can be demanding in its own right. It requires complete physical and personal engagement at the same time as requiring intense concentration on the matter in hand. I had some informal experience to that effect before embarking on what became of my more planned methods exercises. In realising a modest personal ambition, I took a series of lessons in Argentine tango. Being an experienced ethnographer, I – of course – made field notes. I have included extracts from those notes in one of my publications (Atkinson 2020, pp. 38–46, 78–79), and here I summarise some relevant aspects of that mixture of work and leisure.

There is nothing more truly embodied than the attempt to learn how to dance, unless it be participation in sport or exercise such as yoga. To dance together with others is the epitome of thick participation. As an ethnographic exercise, it calls for a fully embodied engagement with others and with the physical tasks in hand. The experience of dance encapsulates the search for embodied knowledge, for rhythm and for the capacity to follow instructions (Broth and Keevallik 2014).

My lessons were in Argentinean tango: not in 'ballroom', that is. It is a distinction that is carefully maintained, the latter being seen as an exaggeratedly distorted version of the original dance. Like several of my other activities, tango was opportunistic. Very near my home in Cardiff, there is a deconsecrated church that has been converted in a community arts and performance centre. A course in tango was advertised. I was sufficiently interested to enrol, planning to take the lessons. My friend, and colleague, Dr Maggie Gregory, also enrolled. As we discovered, going with a partner was more valuable for company and moral support than learning to dance together. The tango classes helped me to focus on the nature of embodied inquiry, although they were undertaken for fun. I had no 'research' purpose, although given who we are, Maggie and I both kept 'field notes' of the classes.

We arrive for our first lesson, joining a gaggle of people waiting for the class to begin. I was relived to see that some of our classmates were no younger or more elegant that I was. The space, created out of a part of the former church, had a wooden floor, and a large mirror on one wall. The mirror became intermittently intimidating, as I glimpsed my less than feline body reflected back during the first and subsequent classes. And so we gathered, about twenty-eight of us; as the evening progressed, the room felt more and more crowded as we started to move. There was a good deal of bumping and apologising.

The basic movement – which our teachers demonstrated – is a walk. It is not just any 'walk', though. The movement is more of a 'slide', on the balls of the feet, the ankles just brushing each other as each foot comes through. So the first movement for the class was to walk round the room in a circle. We were directed to go round the room anticlockwise, because tango is always danced socially in that direction. (This was the first of many appeals to authenticity, couched in terms of how tango is danced in a real *milonga*.) And so we all shuffled round the room, with me trying to walk as instructed, gliding forward, the ankles brushing, steadily and with controlled movements. It seemed very hard to establish a basic tempo or rhythm. Some people seemed to be walking at racing pace, lapping me as they sped round the room.

Soon we were told to take our partners, or to find one if we had come alone. People sorted themselves out quickly. We were told to adopt the 'practice position'. That is, chest-to-chest and face-to-face with arms resting on arms rather than the full embrace that is so characteristic of the tango. We started to practise the walk – men waling forwards, women backwards. Maggie and I did our best, not altogether successfully. I seemed to lurch rather than walking smoothly forward. I was hesitating and then thrusting a leg forward, so I think I was throwing Maggie off balance. As a consequence, our progress was jerky, to my right, her left, instead of moving evenly and gracefully round the room. We were not alone. Some couples looked as though they had danced together before and moved together fairly easily – if not yet idiomatically. Others seemed rooted to the spot and were looking anxious. My ineptitude was a source of chagrin; the clumsiness of others provided some comfort.

In some ways the tango is extremely rhythmic, indeed its rhythms seem to invite sensual movement. But in practice, it is very different from the kind of strict tempo that accompanies ballroom dancing. Picking up the rhythm and responding to the nuances of rubato is not straightforward in tango. In retrospect, I seemed to be 'dancing' to a dotted rhythm, hesitating on the beat. The result was the opposite of the sinuous movement I harboured on my mind's eye. Eventually, we moved to the embrace position, demonstrated by our teachers. They emphasised that tango is danced body-to-body, chest-to-chest, the men's right hand firmly but gently on the woman's back, his left arm extended so that she can just lightly rest her hand on his. The man looks over his partner's right shoulder so that he can lead and guide; this also avoids intrusive eye contact. Our teachers explained more about leading: because tango does not consist of set routines, the couple need to be responsive to the man's lead. This should, we were told, be done in a subtle way, as if one were leading a blind friend to a chair or to a place in a room. It calls for the most gentle of pressure from the hand and a shift in body weight.

Kathy Davis (2015) has published ethnographically on tango, and presents an idealised view of the dance:

Dancing tango requires more than an embodied connection with the music...it involves two bodies coming together in an embrace. The embrace is what sets tango apart from other couple dances in which partners dance on their own or follow each other's movements without actually touching. (p. 57)

It sounds almost idyllic, and when it works for experienced dancers, it seems to be so. But for the novice, it is far from straightforward. From time to time, my partner and I headed in almost completely different directions, or when I did manage to 'lead' her, it was into other couples.

As we practised, I moved to another partner. Compared to me, she seemed to have even less sense of rhythm or movement. As I attempted to lead us, and indeed to get us moving at all, she merely shifted her weight uneasily from foot to foot. I could not tell, of course, whether it was a result of my poor leading, her discomfort at dancing backwards or her response to me as a partner. All are possible and indeed likely. I must admit that there was little that was catlike about my movements, or hers. Something a good deal more stolid and less graceful would be a more appropriate simile. Kathy Davis again:

> The embrace may be the starting point, but in order to be able to dance, partners have to find a way to communicate with each other. Tango requires a constant dialogue – a dialogue without words. (Davis 2015, p. 61)

There is little 'communication' possible between me and my class partners. We have barely mastered the ability to walk, we fail to do so in a coordinated fashion, and we have no shared sense of rhythm.

Later in this first class, the teachers showed us a basic pattern. The man's first movement to the left, bringing his right foot through, walking forward again with the left, bringing the right foot up to join the left, finally moving his right foot to the right. In practice, it generates a pleasingly graceful movement, it being more 'dance' than 'walk'. It is easier to generate some sort of rhythmic movement to the music. At the point we had to try it, my partner was someone it turned out I could dance with; or rather, we were able to dance together in a simple way. She and I were able to establish some rhythm, and although my movements were not as smooth as they should have been, they felt as if they were getting better. There was perhaps a brief moment or two when we might be said to have been dancing.

Different partners make a very big difference. Being focused on my own performance, I am not very successful at leading my partners, and in any case it would be ridiculous to expect even adequate performance after so short an introduction to the dance. But it is very difficult to concentrate on leading one's partner, trying to mesh two bodies into one series of movements. I was certainly self-conscious in doing it, and also aware of a distinct (if trivial) responsibility. If I cannot lead nicely, then my partner cannot enjoy the experience, and – more importantly – she is not going to get the chance to learn tango properly. And when it did not work well, the result could be thoroughly frustrating. There was one young woman with whom I 'danced' with absolutely no success. She resisted every attempt on my part to lead us and instead of dancing chest-to-chest kept pulling away from me veering to her left. The consequence was more of a tussle than a dance, compounded by what seemed to be her total lack of a sense of rhythm.

> When tango works, it creates a unique connection. Dancers' bodies not only have to fit together in terms of their size and posture; they are required to move together in response to the music. (Davis 2015, p. 65)

Such grappling with a stranger reinforces the realisation of physical intimacy. Any sense of what Goffman called civil inattention – not engaging in overt inspection or attention towards another – is quite impossible. Nonetheless, direct mutual gaze is to be avoided in the context of social dancing with a series of partners or in a class like ours. Close physical intimacy was, however, a 'noticeable' feature of the class, as the room got pretty hot: both members of a couple were likely to be a bit sweaty.

As the series of lessons progressed, it became apparent that, of course, there was much more to leading at tango than a matter of steady progress forwards. A young couple of experienced tango dancers came to demonstrate to us. Starting from simple steps, they progressed to more florid moves. There was much more backward movement and circling. At a more modest level, we added further movements. From the simple walk, we learned the 'cross': men slide forward, leading with their chest, turn at an angle to their partners and bring her back into the line of the dance. The female partner reverses backwards. We performed the cross with different partners. I was pleased when my next partner off the 'taxi rank' was the young woman who had demonstrated to us. I was hoping that doing it with someone experienced at tango would enhance my own performance. Unfortunately it did not. We began together but almost immediately she stopped dead. 'That was a very bad cross', she said. It was becoming difficult anyway as there was a mass of couples barging into each other and into us. But we tried again. I think I was leading her very badly, failing to bring her back to our line of dance and then tugging at her. It was a rather crushing experience. At the time, it seemed starkly discouraging, although in principle a valuable lesson. It was yet another reminder that I was *not* leading decisively. I was still not using my chest properly, and was turning my whole chest away from my partner, which was throwing us out of alignment. I realised the need to keep my upper body at the proper angle, then bringing my chest round and then bringing round my partner before I perform the backward step, so that she can step across me and then step back. I realised that if I move my torso properly, then my feet and my partner will follow. If I move my feet first, followed by my body, then my poor partner is always trying to catch up with my feet. So I clearly need to work on the alignment of my body – not just my 'chest' but my shoulders as well.

Learning got a bit more complicated again in a subsequent lesson when we tried to learn the *reverse ocho*, to complement the *forward ocho* we had supposedly learned the previous week. For a man, there is a slow side-to-side effect. The man is creating the space for his partner to perform her *ocho*. As one tries to glide from foot to foot, the motion is akin to the appearance of ice-skating. But as we began to practise it, I immediately started to go wrong, leading off on the wrong foot and failing to achieve the right movement. And as we practised it with partners, I had no idea how many such moves we were expected to perform, or how to come out of a series of *ochos*, as one cannot continue in that way indefinitely. Like so many things, the *reverse ocho* is frustrating. Demonstrated by our teachers, it appears to be simple. In practice, it seems to be hard to accomplish in a properly rhythmic and physically controlled way, no doubt because of its very simplicity.

I continued to attend lessons, with similar results: haltingly accomplishing some of the basic moves, but then forgetting how I had accomplished them by the time the next lesson came round. What I did learn was the importance of physical things, such as posture, and performative issues such as rhythm, tempo and repetition. To make even an approximation of dancing tango, one has to try to manage the body in an appropriate way. It requires a tango posture, and a way of moving that resembles that of the accomplished dancer: sinuous movement, the foot moving parallel to the floor, the torso bent slightly forward into one's partner. It is easy to observe in others, fairly easy to understand in principle, harder to achieve and sustain. Attempting to achieve tango means placing oneself physically into the world in a particular way. It is a style of physical being. It requires the 'right' kind of physical *posture*. It requires a practical grasp of choreography, in the sense of managing one's own and one's partner's movements in the physical and social space of the studio. I never acquired sufficient competence to become 'beautiful' (Bosse 2015), but I did become conscious of the need to modify my body in the attempt to become a dancer.

As we shall see, these are early lessons in embodied ethnography that carry on through the more sustained methodological exercises that follow. In the dance studio, choreography and the techniques of the body are perhaps self-evident. But they are features of other studios too. In the craft studio, the management of the body – posture and gesture – are fundamentally important. So too is the figure of repetition. Actions are not learned individually and serially. They have to be acquired and practised as a whole, as a Gestalt of embodied sequences. Learning is not a cognitive accomplishment, or not primarily so. It depends upon a variety of physical and sensory engagements. Hence, in microcosm, each new activity of learning encapsulates aspects of ethnographic work. Practical ethnography necessarily implies our physical presence in a social world – in physical, sensory and imaginative ways. We respond to the rhythms, the temporal sequences of everyday life and work. While we do not seek to become fully enculturated experts, we do our work partly through mimetic means. We observe the distinctive ways of others' practices: how they move through time and space; how they talk: how they do things with things. We learn through observation, but also through a more incarnate sense of what it takes to act in that way. We come to understand style, grace and skilful performance.

3

Hot Glass: Embodied Learning

The London Glassblowing Studio is near where I have a home in London, in Bermondsey. For most of my life Bermondsey, on the south bank of the Thames, was not the sort of place that one visited (except perhaps for the Friday morning antiques market). In recent decades, it has become very different. Bermondsey Street, where the glass studio is located, is now an upmarket place of restaurants, bars, the outpost of the White Cube art gallery, expensive apartments and a fashion museum. I confess that my first visit to the studio was impromptu and unannounced. I happened to be passing and popped in. Like similar glass studios, it is open to visitors. The frontstage region is a gallery, displaying pieces by the makers who work there. Beyond that is the studio itself, and a small number of chairs invite the visitor to linger for a while and watch the makers at work. The only glass studios I had visited briefly as a tourist were in Seattle, one of the centres of glass-making in the United States. They had much the same layout, which is indeed a common feature of glass shops everywhere.

I sat and watched the makers for a while, and when they paused in their work I spoke to a couple of them, and asked if Peter Layton was available. They said he was. I waited. Peter Layton is the owner and master craftsman of the studio, and I knew that to be the case. Peter appeared, and we had a short conversation. I explained myself briefly. I usually describe my interests in terms of 'anthropology' rather than 'sociology'. The former seems to sound more intriguing, and does reflect my disciplinary background. I explained very briefly my interest in craft and makers, and Peter responded very positively, and added that if I really wanted to understand glass-making then I really ought to sign up for one of their introductory classes. I agreed that it sounded like a good idea.

Studio glass in the United Kingdom is relatively recent. Studio potters like Bernard Leach had a stock of skills, techniques and equipment to draw on, whereas pioneers of glass had to develop their studios from scratch. There were of course tools and techniques in glass-making from

Murano and factories elsewhere. But the pioneers had to work out how to scale down furnaces and processes from factory scale to smaller studios. Peter Layton was a pioneer in British studio glass, working in that style from the late 1960s (Layton 1996, 2006). Layton established London Glassblowing in Rotherhithe (South London) in 1976. The studio then moved to premises at Leathermarket in Bermondsey (also south of the River) and in 2009, it moved to its present home in Bermondsey Street, remaining in a neighbourhood in London that has become gentrified round it since that time. Sustaining studio glass-making is not easy in the current commercial climate, given that cheap copies of glass designs can be manufactured very cheaply in China and sold by home-furnishing stores and departments. The London Glass-blowing studio has succeeded in resisting the economic trends that have impinged on craft-based hand-made glass, which include not just competition from cheap imports but also steeply rising costs of premises and energy (needed to keep furnaces going). London Glassblowing is the home of a team of highly talented artists, who contribute to making Layton's own designs, and make their own individual pieces. For biographies of those glass artists, see *Past and Present: Peter Layton and London Glassblowing* (Layton 2012).

Glass-making is one of those crafts with a long history, and many of the techniques and tools are time honoured, as is the layout of the studio itself. Discussions of the craft often make reference to the tradition of glass-making in Venice: on the island of Murano, to be precise. The Venetian glass-makers were banished to the island as long ago as the thirteenth century because their furnaces kept causing fires in the densely packed buildings of Venice. The makers of Murano have used the same tools for centuries, and they are one important reference point for glass-making traditions and authenticity. Modern and contemporary artists – such as the American Dale Chihuly – have taken glass design and sculpture in very different directions. In this chapter, my introduction to glass recapitulates the basics of Murano and subsequent traditions. The craft tradition includes the assemblage of tools, the furnaces and the workbench or seat. The latter is also sometimes referred to as the 'gaffer's chair', being traditionally the preserve of the master craftsman.

I confess that I had not at the time thought of taking a class in glass-making. But it seemed as if taking a class would be a very suitable entrée into the studio. Again, I had not really thought of such classes as methodological exercises in their own right. But as I have explained, that is what happened, and so instead of an extended ethnographic immersion in the glass studio, it became the site for the first of my learning experiences. As I waited for the class to take place I was apprehensive. I have never been 'good with my hands', and any practical making has normally defeated me. I do not relish the heat and danger of glass-making or blacksmithing. I found my secondary school's metal-working shop – with its forge and blowtorches – scary when I was young. More to the point, I did not relish the prospect of making myself look foolish. Participating in a class, however small, could be a recipe for an existential exposure that I did not fancy. After looking into the matter, I knew that each class would last for a day, with four learners and two tutors. The classes took place at the weekend, when the studio was not otherwise in use. The instructions for the day had been clear and simple: 'work' clothes, with a long-sleeved shirt, and closed shoes (no open toes for women). In a clear premonition of the heat of the studio, we were also instructed to bring with us a bottle of water. I knew about the heat of the shop already, of course, having visited it and having harboured some anxieties about the furnaces and the hot glass itself. The 'class' consisted of myself, another man, and two women.

There were two young men in the studio when we arrived. They introduced themselves as Anthony Scala and Layne Rowe. Anthony gave us our introductory talk. He showed us the furnace in the centre of the back wall, holding a reservoir of molten glass at a temperature of about 1,100° (which added to the sense of apprehension). Flanking it were two more furnaces – called 'glory holes' – that are used to re-heat glass that is being worked on. Flanking these in turn were two pipe-heating ovens, where gathering irons and pipes are kept hot, enabling one to work with the molten glass. We were given a protective sleeve to wear (Layne said he had just washed them), and were advised to remove watches and jewellery; I had already taken off my watch and had not put on my usual ring.

Anthony took us through a tour of the hot shop and the safety precautions. Having pointed out the furnaces, he introduced us to some of the basic tools. They included wooden blocks, made of cherry-wood (which is slow burning). Used to shape hot glass, they resemble large, thick ice-cream scoops. Used wet, they are kept in a bucket of water. Then there are the 'jacks' (also *pucellas*), metal tools that resemble a very large pair of tweezers or compasses. Anthony also explained that hot glass can be shaped in the hand, using nothing more than wet newspaper. The hot-shop safety precautions were impressed on us. Anthony said that those of us wearing spectacles would be ok, but otherwise safety glasses would have to be worn, in case of any splashes. He also pointed out that if we were passing behind anyone in the studio we needed to say something like 'Behind you'. As I went on to observe, this is part of a broader choreography of the glass studio, and beyond that, there is an element of choreography in much practical studio work. An illustrated review of glass-making tools can be found in a section based on an interview with Peter Layton in *The Story of Tools*, edited by Mark Hooper (2019).

In the course of the morning session, we made three solid objects. The first was an exercise that seems to be standard in glass-making lessons. It began with a gather of glass from the central furnace. One cannot simply stick a rod into the open furnace door: the gathering rod needs to be angled down into the glass so that a blob can be collected from the crucible within. This means elevating the end in one's hands, so that the far end is dipped into the molten glass. The heat and the glare are extreme. So the novice has little idea how much of a gather has been achieved, and it is partly trial-and-error. It slowly becomes a matter of 'feel', as one develops a surer touch and better capacity to judge whether the tip has gone into the glass properly.

The first three objects we made were apparently standard beginning pieces. The first was a clear glass segmented sausage or caterpillar shape. Having gathered glass, we rolled it to shape on what is called the 'marver' – a steel bench on which glass is rolled, originally in the historical origins of glass-making a marble slab. Having created a plain sausage, we learned how to use jacks to create deep grooves, creating three segments. This meant sitting at the bench or chair, turning the glass at the end of a rod while firmly gripping the jacks and keeping them vertical to the glass. It is not easy, simple though the operation is in principle. As I grip and turn, the pressure I exert is uneven; the jacks slip, the grooves are uneven, and instead of being symmetrical they twist and corkscrew. My segmented glass sausage is a poor specimen. But already I am learning something about how the glass feels, and how to hold a gather of glass on the rod. Having made just one elementary and imperfect piece, the heat of the glass and the strangeness of the whole enterprise starts to seem less troublesome. So far, at least, I have not burned myself, dropped the glass or otherwise made a complete fool of myself.

The two other pieces made in the morning are more satisfying. Each is a 'paperweight': that is, a solid piece of glass. Each gives us the opportunity to add colour to our object. My first is best described as an asymmetric rounded glass pebble. Having gathered sufficient clear glass, I have rolled it in powdered colour on the marver, choosing a bluish purple. It is pleasingly chunky to make, and because there is no set pattern, it cannot be 'wrong'. The second piece is slightly more advanced, being a conical shape, with two colours – red and white – trailed in. Since this is a more definite shape, it calls for more work. The wooden blocks are used to round the glass, while the final conical shape is produced by hand with wet newspaper. It is hard to judge how well the colours have worked until the glass has cooled.

Solid paperweight

In the afternoon, we embark on blowing glass. First, we are to make an open-ended vase-like vessel in clear glass. The first task is to gather sufficient glass, making more than one visit to the furnace. Of course, the novice's question (and one that others always ask) is: how hard do you have to blow? How much air has to go in? For a novice like me, it is a matter of trial-and-error. My first attempt is too timid a puff and has virtually no effect on the glass. But as Layne, my tutor, points out, when the air reaches the hot glass it expands. So one is not having to keep blowing to create the void. Provided you put a thumb over the end of the blowing pipe, the air cannot escape. I manage to create a blown sphere at the end of the pipe. In order to create an open-ended vessel that is then transferred to another rod (a punty), attached by means of a small blob of soft hot glass. The jacks are then used to open out the mouth of the vessel. The aim was to create, in clear glass, a fairly small straight-sided vase, with an even rim. Unfortunately, in the course of twiddling the glass and applying the jacks, I managed to damage the embryonic vessel. It had to be rescued by Layne, but remained a poor thing. It was wobbly and lopsided. It really did not even look like a happy accident, and although of course it was retained and returned to me eventually, after cooling, it should really have been scrapped.

My final piece for the day was a coloured vessel in a design of our own choosing, using whatever colours we wanted. I decided to stick with the red and white I had already used. But this time I wanted the blown vessel to be entirely white, with red stripes. I also wanted it to be encased in clear glass – what the Murano makers call *sommerso* – an idea I had taken from some of the pieces on the display shelves in the gallery part of the studio. Rather to my surprise and delight 'I' succeeded in making it: which is to say that Layne did much of the making, while I really acted as his assistant. Adding the clear glass to encase the vessel transformed the overall appearance of the piece. It also made it much heavier. I realised just how hard it could be to manage a substantial piece of glass when it is at the other end of a longish pipe. It tested my strength and my ability to control the process physically. I failed to make the clear glass – and hence the overall shape of 'my' vessel – symmetrical. But I was relieved to have it and myself in one piece by the end of the afternoon. As well as the intrinsic satisfaction of making some passable glass objects, my thick participation granted me some lessons, specific to the work with glass but – as we shall see – not all confined to the glass studio.

Experiencing glass

At an experiential, phenomenological level, full participation gave me the following insights. First, of course, there is the phenomenon of the heat – although admittedly I would have felt that had I only been observing the scene. The heat is especially powerful when one puts the gathering iron into the furnace to gather glass. One has to stand close to the furnace and one has to look directly into it when making a gather (although my instructor, Layne, stood close to me and told me when I was 'in the glass', as it is quite hard to see exactly where the end of the iron is in relation to the surface of the molten glass). Likewise, standing in front of the glory-hole and holding the pipe horizontal while turning the glass can feel extremely hot. Only once did I feel that the heat was actually uncomfortable and had to resist flinching when I was shaping one of the blown pieces in the afternoon, and the glass itself was very hot. I could feel it lightly burning the skin on my right hand. The heat was radiating directly from the glass itself. It was not really burning me to the extent of blistering my skin, but it certainly felt momentarily uncomfortable. On one or two occasions, my hand strayed too close to the hot end of the pipe but it was not enough actually to burn me. I did notice that two of my fellow students experienced very mild burns.

Secondly, there is the 'feel' of the glass on the pipe. It looks fairly straightforward to keep it turning and thus to keep the glass even. In practice, it is not so straightforward. With a lump of glass on the end of my iron, and heating it in the glory-hole, I am constantly aware of its potential to droop downwards. There are recurrent fears of it slipping off the pipe altogether and falling into the furnace. (What would happen then? I wondered. Luckily it never occurred.) From time to time one stops twiddling in order to let the glass 'centre', but then it can start to droop almost immediately. The glass itself is at once responsive and malleable, yet hard to control, being highly plastic. Likewise, the heat is a resource, making the management of the glass a possibility, yet it creates a somewhat intimidating working environment. The heat and the glare can be intrusive aspects of the immediate environment, reminding us that there is a degree of discomfort or even danger involved. We novices are not accustomed to working in such conditions. One cannot simply reach out to touch the medium. The glass is always being manipulated at (literally) arm's length, except for when one is manipulating it directly with a jack, a block or one's hand through wet paper. But the direct touch of, say, clay is absent. One is also aware of the weight of the glass. When I was making my last piece, which had a fairly chunky amount of glass encasing my blown glass interior, successive gathers meant that I ended up with a large amount of glass, which, given the length of the blowing pipe, was hard to control and to support at arm's length. I had to confess to Layne that I was having difficulty managing the weight.

Also, hands-on participation means that I was able to sense shaping the glass with the tools and also with a pad of newspaper. I could feel the resistance of the glass as it cools – it seems to go rapidly from being so soft it is in danger of slipping off the pipe altogether, to becoming quite stiff and intractable in a short space of time. It is, of course, for this reason, that it needs to go into the glory-hole repeatedly while one is working on it. There is something extremely satisfying in the weight of the glass as one works on it. It has a very considerable physical presence in its own right. On the other hand, the full participation as a student means that one's concentration is almost exclusively on the practical accomplishment of the task in hand. Given the nature of glass-work, full concentration is vital. Losing control of the glass can ruin the making process. It can also, of course, be dangerous not to concentrate fully in such a hot and potentially dangerous shop-floor environment. It is not, however, my main intention to focus on the personal and experiential nature of my preliminary encounter with hot glass. Such experiences are only valuable insofar as they provide insight into and illuminate more general features of social phenomena. Here, therefore, I turn to a more thematic presentation. The following sections therefore summarise key features of the process of making, and of the pedagogy that reproduces that process.

Even in the course of this short introductory exercise, I could start to feel, as well as observe, the 'flow' of the embodied work (Jackson 2011). As O'Connor (2007a) writes of her novice glass-blowing, of gathering the glass and blowing a vessel (a goblet):

> Though my technical ability enabled my gather, I did not pay heed
> to each step, the distinctness of which had been insisted upon in my

early days of glassblowing, but rather attended the gather itself, the correctness of which informed, if necessary, immediate adjustments in my techniques. I knew my gathering had been apt by virtue of the gather (p. 130).

I did not gain such practical competence, and would not expect to, but I could certainly sense what it would be like: to intend and carry out an *action* (such as gathering the glass) rather than a series of separate tasks (such as holding the pipe correctly, inserting into the molten glass, removing it, keeping it turning, and so on).

The quality of the glass

The glass is an intrinsically beautiful and aesthetically pleasing medium to work with. When it glows with an inner fire, and of course, as one works and shapes it, one feels both its mass and its smooth surface. One picks up brightly coloured minerals – powdered or crystalline – that are then transformed in the process of working the glass. When they are hot, the colours of the glass can only be surmised or predicted from experience. In this glass is akin to glazed pottery, which must be waited for until it has been fired in the kiln. The glass must be put in the annealing oven and cooled over a period of time. For our pieces the cooling period would be just a day or two. Antony explained that for some large and complex pieces the cooling period could be months. But the exact outcome of the colours cannot be known until the pieces are taken out at the end of the cooling period – just as the potter cannot finally know the outcome of glazing and firing until the kiln is cool and opened. Deferred gratification can be an intrinsic aspect of much craft and artistic work.

My *sommerso* vessel

Angles

The skills I am trying to learn involve *working the angles*. There are various aspects to the process of making – gathering, controlling, rolling, getting the glass off the pipe, adding colour, blowing – that are determined, or at least facilitated by getting the angles right. To start at the beginning: if one takes the iron or the pipe from the glory hole – where its tip has been heating – then there are ways of carrying towards the furnace that are controlled and safe. One does not wave it around, or trail it. It is carried, something like a pole-vaulter's pole, at a steep angle in front of the body and in front of the eyes. As one approaches the open door of the furnace, then the end is lifted (again, like planting a pole) the pipe is rested on the bottom of the opening, and the tip of the pipe introduced into the molten glass. When the glass has been collected, then the pipe is removed, and still turning, now kept on the level. When one takes the glass to the marver to roll it, then again the angle of attack is significant. To coat a lump of glass with powdered colour evenly all over, it has to be rolled in the colour horizontally, but then to coat the far end, the proximal end of the pipe needs to be raised, so that the tip of the glass is rolling in the colour; then the pipe may need to be lowered, so that the end nearest the pipe is also coated. One may need to lower the glass (still turning), so that the glass starts to come off the pipe. (It is not the purpose to have the glass coating the pipe, but of course ultimately it needs to come off the pipe, so the less glass actually on the tip the better.) During blowing, the glass may be lowered and twiddled. We were shown how to blow seated on the bench, leaning back and blowing with the pipe resting on the arm of the workbench. So the angle of the pipe is downwards. Throughout the process, therefore, the angle of the pipe is crucial in controlling the glass itself, as it is in the process of shaping and colouring it. Using the wooden blocks is also dependent on getting various angles right – for instance, applying pressure with the block at a slight angle, so as to create a 'shoulder' in the glass at the end of the pipe.

Getting a feel

As I have suggested already, getting the right angles is also dependent on having (or not having) a feel for the glass and for the tools. This is especially evident at the beginning of the day. Our first hands-on task was designed to introduce us to several elementary things. We collected a small amount of glass and then rolled it on the marver, producing a sausage-like shape. Taking it from the marver to the work-bench, via the glory-hole, we then used the piece to practise hands-on use of the jacks. Our initial task was to use those to create two grooves in the rod, to create a series of rounded shapes. This is, therefore, an exercise in using the jacks. But, as a novice, one has no idea of how hard to press. Again, it is partly a matter of getting the angles right. The tool should be held firmly in one hand, vertically. I learned, as quickly as I could, not to apply too much pressure. But equally, I discovered that if one does not have the jacks at the right angle, or with the right pressure, then it can easily slip on the glass, especially as it cools and becomes less tractable. If it moves, then one can inadvertently create a corkscrew-like effect rather than a straight groove. Likewise, applying the various sized wood blocks requires a certain feel: the angle at which the block is held to the glass makes a difference. It is hard to judge what pressure to apply, not least because the pressure is exerted from below. We are not necessarily used to pushing upwards quite like that. The same is true of using the tool to make flat sides and angles. It is hard to judge how much pressure to apply. The glass is resistant, and the right amount of pressure is not easy to estimate. And as we have seen, how much, how hard, or how long to blow? The effect of blowing is not instantaneous. How hard is it to get the air into the glass? Is it like starting to blow up a balloon, requiring a lot of puff to overcome initial resistance? Does it require a steady, extended breath, or a brief burst? Layne demonstrated, this aspect, telling us to breathe from the chest (just like opera singers, I thought at the time) and not to puff hard from our cheeks. He also said he found it a good idea to stop the mouthpiece with his thumb, otherwise the breath can be dissipated, and it can be controlled more that way, while the trapped air expands naturally within the hot glass.

One's sense of working the angles is intimately related to the use of tools. For the novice like me, the tools themselves, which are aesthetically pleasing in their own right, are alien objects. Indeed, there are, as it were, always two elements in any action that need to be controlled – the hot glass and the tool. The apprentice who is committed to learning and practising glassblowing 'properly' needs to acquire a sense of the tool as an extension of her or his embodied self:

> To feel through tools is to extend ourselves into and embody those tools. Embodiment, or extension of our corporeal bodies through things, permeates our everyday experience – through a pen, the texture of paper, through shoes' soles, the give of ground underneath ... our lived body is much more than our own flesh and blood: our body reaches out and inhabits a phenomenological domain. The lived phenomenological character of our corporeal experience allows the novice foremost to come into contact with the glass through an extension of herself through the tools, a relation without which the practical knowledge of glassblowing cannot develop. (O'Connor 2006, p. 182)

The guiding hand

The rhetoric that informed the day's instruction was couched in terms of 'us' making our pieces – especially the last piece. The first four were prescribed by the instructors, and obviously most of the day follows a set pattern: apart from anything else, the timing of the day seems to be pretty predictable, based on those initial student pieces. But the last piece was up to us. We were encouraged to look round the gallery shelves and identify something we would like to make (or at least get some ideas from them). There is no doubt that we all 'made' our pieces, in the sense that we physically gathered the glass, physically rolled it on the marver, we sat at the workbench and held the blocks and the jacks. But we succeeded in 'making' the pieces because of the instructor's guiding hand. He made sure that our irons were at the right angle; he guided us in holding the blocks; he helped us to judge how hard to hold the jacks; he made sure that our dollop of glass was under control, physically taking control of the iron. Although we sat at the workbench, the instructor had a good deal of control over what we were doing. As well as giving verbal advice, therefore, there was a strong guiding hand. Explicit advice and physical support combined to ensure that we actually made the pieces more or less as intended, that we did not commit any major disasters, and minor problems of performance were coped with. I made one of the latter. In order to release a piece from the iron, one needs to score a groove with the jacks, and – all being well – a sharp tap on the pipe will release the vessel. But when we were making my first blown vessel – the straight-sided vase in clear glass – I tapped a little too vigorously and it didn't come away cleanly, and part of the end shattered. Together we improvised re-shaping the piece to be asymmetrical, putting the glass back in the glory hole and softening the jagged edge into a more 'meant' shape. I used the jacks to open the vessel out a bit to create a gently flaring lip at the same time. So between us we improvised a rescue of sorts.

My final piece was satisfying, but illustrates how Layne really made the piece, while I did some of the purely mechanical aspects. I decided I wanted to make a 'chunky' bowl, and I indicated something on the shelf that was, in general terms, the 'sort of thing' I had in mind. We were allowed to choose what colours we wanted to use. I decided I wanted to use opaque white as a block colour, with a trail of red over it. That meant that I rolled my sausage of glass in the white powder that Layne had spread over the marver, but he had to make the red trail to apply over my white glass. The consequence was that on a couple of occasions we had our irons in the glory hole simultaneously. Back at the work-bench, I turned my piece of glass while Layne applied the red trail. It became extremely heavy, to the extent that the weight of the glass went over from being a source of satisfaction to being quite troublesome. It became physically difficult for me to manage the glass properly. (Since the actual glass vessel was not really all that big, this was useful insight into the real weight of the genuinely large pieces that are made in the studio, and that I have subsequently observed in the making.)

Posture

From time to time throughout the day, and in retrospect, I realised how important are one's bodily posture and the techniques of the body (cf. O'Connor 2007b). I realise of course that this is a key aspect of socialised competence in virtually any activity. I realised, for instance, that while I was heating my glass in the glory-hole, I was unnecessarily hunched. My shoulders were raised and were unhelpfully taut. I therefore tried to modify my stance at the glory-hole, adopting a more relaxed posture. It was understandable that I should be tense. I am entirely unaccustomed to working physically, and especially unused to working with such hot (and potentially dangerous) materials. Equally, quite apart from the heat, there is a need to be precise in managing the glass. As I have already suggested, there is a premium to getting the angles right, and part of that resides in one's physical comportment. Holding the iron or the pipe at the right angle (for marvering, for instance) is aided by an appropriate stance. If the end of the iron needs to be raised or lowered (in order to roll out the glass, or to pick up one or more colours) then one can get into ungainly postures. Rather than, say, bending one's knees to lower the iron, it is easy to stoop from the waist and to hunch over the work. Of course, this does not render the work impossible, but it has several consequences. In the first place, poor posture is tiring. When the glass is heavy, then poor posture makes it even more difficult to manage the iron. It also leads to backache. Secondly, it can make for clumsy movement. Rolling glass on the marver needs to be done smoothly. If it is jerky, then it is all too easy to create a flat surface or spot on the glass instead of creating a smoothly rounded piece of glass. (In that case, it can be reheated in the glory-hole, of course, so it is not a disaster.) Thirdly, if one's movement is clumsy or restricted it can make it hard to keep working the glass consistently, so it can get droopy and off-centre. Working the angles, therefore, depends on one's physical self-management.

Choreography

Closely related to posture is the choreography of making. Safe and productive work in the hot shop requires a certain kind of choreography.

By that I mean smooth and effective movement. One approaches the furnace in order to gather glass. The iron is already hot, so one transports with care, bearing it with as much confidence as one can, and avoiding letting it wave around. Likewise there is a choreography of taking the iron and a gather of glass to the chair to work on it. One has to keep it turning and keep the glass controlled. One has to pass one's body between the iron and the chair itself, while putting the iron down, resting on both arms of the chair. For the most part Layne took my iron while I was sitting down, so that the most tricky little manoeuvre was resolved: nevertheless, the actual transfer from the marver to the chair, via the glory-hole required a certain amount of physical co-ordination. Sitting or standing to blow the glass also requires a degree of choreographic co-ordination. The practised use of the body and an appropriate posture, coupled with a smooth handling of the iron allows one to blow pre-dictably and in a controlled way. One can also inspect the bubble, in order to gauge how much blowing is required, with good management of the iron and the body.

Alchemy and magic

There are many things about the process of making glass that are 'magical'. Most notably, there is the entire process whereby a blob, or several blobs, of glass are transformed, through the repeated application of elementary techniques, into the many shapes and colours of the finished piece. Then there are the deceptively simple steps in that process – a notable example being the swinging of an open blown vessel to create a flared, 'handkerchief' vessel. Likewise, spinning a vessel to produce a flattened, platter shape, is a magical, if simple, procedure that transforms a basic blown vessel into a new shape. Equally, of course, there is the magic of the colours – the way the glass and the pigments interact to create swirls and patches of coloured vessels. For the novice, this is all but mysterious. For the experienced maker, it is much more controlled. On subsequent visits to the studio I have watched the makers create pieces that reproduce the colours and designs of studio pieces with considerable control and skill. The studio has at any given time a series of designs, differently shaped vessels that are based on combinations of colours. In repeating those vessels, the makers are not trying to create exactly the same patterns of colour in the glass, but they do know how to create the effects. In other words, they are working with 'precedents' as I have called them, rather than working with exact designs they try to replicate.

   There is a strong sense of the alchemy that takes place in the hot-glass studio. Base materials (such as the ingredients of glass itself) are transformed through the fire and through the craft-knowledge of the glass-maker into variously shaped and vividly coloured vessels that seem to transcend their mundane origins, and the repetitious practices that generate such exotic objects. This is an object-lesson in the fact that it does not require mysteriously exotic techniques to generate exotic outcomes. In this context I use the term alchemy advisedly. Although it has anachronistic overtones of quackery, early modern alchemy was indistinguishable in many ways from 'science', as it was from the practical crafts. The alchemists gave us not gold from base materials, but something almost as good, porcelain ('white gold'), dyes, and other laboratory products. Glass itself pre-dates alchemy, of course. But, together with metal-working, it shares the same magical properties: the ordinary, the dull, the mundane is transformed through the fire and by the skilled hands and eyes of the maker into something beautiful, precious and unique. Alchemy is something I shall return to. Implicitly and sometimes explicitly it is present in all of the activities I comment on: how simple base materials and some elementary procedures can be transformed into something new, special and unique. It is a recurring theme here because I want to stress the alchemical nature of ethnographic practice itself.

Like several of the projects in this book hot glass implies deferred gratification. Each object must cool slowly. It has to be placed in an oven, where the temperature is reduced in a controlled way. If it cools too quickly it will crack. Also, the colours in the glass cannot be seen and appreciated properly until it has cooled. So one must wait a while. While it is hot and while it is still cooling, of course, one cannot handle a piece, appreciate its weight, volume, colours or surface. Two weeks after my class I went back to collect my pieces. As I expected, two of my pieces – the sausage and the lame blown vase – were pretty bad. But I was pleased with the other three, and my final piece was especially gratifying, if a bit clumsy.

Now, as I have noted, I am not the only ethnographer to have learned some lessons of the studies through glassblowing. Mine, as I have described, was an aliquot of fieldwork, a very brief methodological exercise. By contrast, Erin O'Connor has followed a far more extended apprenticeship and has published a series of papers derived from her work. I have not embedded reference to her work hitherto in this chapter. That is not because I want to marginalise her work: far from it. Rather, I want to make a very particular and explicit comparison between O'Connor's ethnographic experience and my own. There are some very clear parallels between the New York studio studied by O'Connor and the London studio I visited.

A comparison of my own text with O'Connor's reveals some striking parallels. The most obvious reflect the material circumstances of the glassblowing studios. This is not remarkable in itself – but does reflect the extent to which the basic set-up of a hot-glass studio is constant over time and space. The physical arrangement of the studio and the basic tools are the same. The nomenclature is the same. As I have said, this is not in itself a particularly striking observation, as we know from descriptions and illustrations that the glass studio has remained essentially unchanged for centuries: the glory-holes and the furnace containing the molten glass, the marver and the workbench, the furnace containing the molten glass, the jacks and the wooden blocks – these are all stable, recurrent elements in the history of the craft. So it is not surprising that the New York and London studios have the same mise-en-scene. What is more informative, however, is the close similarity between the pedagogic events as I describe them and as O'Connor does.

O'Connor's classes were spread over a longer period than my one-day class (which lasted eight hours, including a one-hour lunch break). She writes graphically about the 'warmth' of the glass and the sensory, embodied response to the heat of the glass, translated into a practical appreciation of its technical possibilities. She describes the use of the jacks in making a 'caterpillar' shape, learning to make the grooves in the soft glass, noting that while it sounds easy it is not as the novice lacks the embodied sense of its accomplishment and cannot envisage the outcomes of specific activities. Striving to jack appropriate grooves, heating and re-heating the glass, the novice learns the significance of heat, as well as the practical manipulation of the jacks themselves. Although she does not express it in quite the same terms as I do, O'Connor also discusses angles. For instance, she develops a discussion of the use of the jacks; referring to a close-up photograph of a glassblower's work, she says:

> ....the glassblower is likely rotating the glass towards him, riding the front of the bubble at the bubble's set angle with the jacks by tilting his wrist out and downwards, so that he pulls the glass towards him as he rotates (2007c, p. 72).

It is clear from our respective accounts that the basic, introductory training followed the same pattern. Indeed, as novices we both made the same object – the 'caterpillar' (as O'Connor calls it – it remained unnamed during my lesson). Moreover, and this is where the pedagogy of craft and the craft of ethnography converge, we describe similar experi- ences in the making of the piece itself, and of working physically with the glass. This in turn suggests something that goes beyond just a 'first days in the field' in one glass studio. There is clearly every reason to believe that in addition to the physical arrangements and the tools of glass-making, there is a pedagogy of training that is itself stable. Now this should not surprise us. There are many examples of art, craft and performance in which the forms and contents of pedagogy are remarkably stable. Novices progress through basic exercises and learn techniques in set patterns and routines in many types of artistic and artisanal activity. In this respect the training situation is analogous to the master-class in the performing arts (cf. Atkinson, Delamont and Watermeyer 2012; Atkinson 2013a, b) at the other end of the spectrum of ability and experience. It is not unlike the initial exposure to school science that we also described in terms of the ubiquity of the Bunsen burner (Delamont, Beynon and Atkinson 1988). The pedagogy of the glass studio is an intensely practical one. It is predicated on the physical mastery of some elementary materials, tools and techniques. It is accomplished most exclusively through (literally) hands-on making. The pedagogy is thus, in part, inscribed in the material arrangements of the studio, and is couched in terms of those physical competences that the tools and techniques call for. There is little or no room for alternative approaches, or for novelty. There are tried-and-trusted routines that are part of the shared culture of the craft. Moreover, they work: the physical artefacts that are produced by the end of the training day are concrete testimony to the efficacy of the training. The pedagogy of the studio is therefore predicated not on the learner – it is not student-centred in that sense – and it is not teacher-centred either. It is 'centred' on techniques, tools and materials. Its embodiment lies not just in the physical bodies of the students and teachers, but is equally embodied in the materials and the physical arrangements of the studio itself.

In other words, there is something especially stable in the craft of glass-making, as there is in the pedagogy of glass-blowing classes. As I have noted already, and as the teachers at the London Glassblowing Studio emphasised, there is a long, continuous tradition embedded in the material arrangements of the studio. The physical surroundings, the tools, the techniques – these have been visibly part of glass-working technology for centuries. They are stable over time and in space: the glassblowers of Murano use precisely the same tools, sitting in the same chairs, as their counterparts in London, and – as O'Connor's ethnography makes clear – in New York also. There is, of course, a yet greater stability at stake here. That is, stability of the ethnographic enterprise itself. We do not have to subscribe to narrow definitions of validity or reliability to appreciate the values of multiple or repeated studies. It is rare for ethnographic research to be undertaken specifically in order to replicate previous studies. That was certainly not my intention in embarking on my study of glassblowing, which – as I have indicated already – was grounded in my much wider interest in craft studios. To that extent, therefore, the convergence between my own fieldwork and that of O'Connor was fortuitous. O'Connor developed her work into a much more extended ethnography than I have reported in this paper, which is based on my own experience as a learner on an introductory course. But these convergences are testimony to the robustness of the ethnographic gaze. The pedagogy of the studio and the ethnography of the studio together reflect the continuity and stability of the *forms* of work: the configuration of material resources; the affordances of the glass itself; the recurrent forms of glass vessels; the techniques of blowing and shaping the glass. In the same way, the forms of ethnographic inference can reflect the affordances of participation and observation: the ability to transform the base materials of observation into analyses that transcend the particularities of the here and now, and to speak to generic themes of social action, organisation and knowledge.

4

Clay: Tools and Turnings

Clay: throwing

In this and the following chapter, I continue my accounts of craft-based learning with examples drawn from ceramics, wood-working and silversmithing. This chapter is devoted to working with clay – specifically my introduction to throwing and turning pots. Here I concentrate on materials, tools and techniques, exploring further what can be gleaned from an aliquot of fieldwork. I base this chapter on two days in a London ceramics studio. Just as was the case with glass-making, working with clay – and subsequently wood and metal – meant I had to grapple with unfamiliar materials and tools. Each of those settings raised issue of physical embodiment, posture and engagement with materials, mediated by the use of tools. Therefore, yet again we find ourselves engaging with issues that Marcel Mauss gathered under the umbrella of 'technique'. For a learner or apprentice in such studios, technique is more or less everything. Mastery of tools and materials, and the coordination of the body with them, are required. Precision in all of that is indispensable.

I had already made several visits to Chris Keenan's studio in south London, watching him making pots, and I had also visited on studio open days. He shares the studio with another potter, Carina Ciscato. They share their studio in Vanguard Court, which is a collection of old out-buildings, on a cobbled walk, behind a former piano factory. The units, of various shapes and sizes, are used by makers and artists in many ways. On collective open days, one can spend hours visiting the studios, talking to the makers, and – of course – buying precious things, including stained glass, ceramics and jewellery. Chris, he had explained to me, was apprenticed to Edmund de Waal, a highly significant British ceramic artist and author (e.g. de Waal 2010, 2011, 2015). Like de Waal, Chris uses a severely restricted range of materials. He only pots in Limoges porcelain, and uses few glazes – often a pale jade-green celadon and an iron-rich brown tenmoku. The two complement each other perfectly, and evoke many 'traditional' ceramics. De Waal himself is even more severe, using only a white glaze for his porcelain. Of his own work, de Waal (2015) writes:

> If you make things out of porcelain clay, you exist in the present moment. My porcelain comes from Limoges in the Limousin region of France, halfway down on the West. It comes in twenty-kilo bags, each bag with two ten-kilo sausages of perfectly blended porcelain clay, the colour of full-fat milk, with a bloom of green mould. (p. 3)

I therefore inherited a severely classical approach in porcelain.

By the time I tried hands-on practical experience, I had undertaken classes in several of the other crafts written about in this book, and I was keen to learn a little about clay. The contents of this book do not follow the chronology of my learning experiences. I had visited Chris's studio early on in my encounters with craft-artists, but took a class from him considerably later. Chris did not seem to offer regular classes at his studio, so I asked him to recommend a teacher. In the event, he offered to tutor me himself. He agreed to let me have a two-day course, one-to-one: day one throwing pots, and day two turning them. (The significance of turning will become apparent as the chapter unfolds.) That was an excellent outcome, as I could have hands-on experience in a studio I had already visited, with a potter I already knew pretty well: I had already bought a small number of Chris Keenan's pots. There is a world of difference between watching a maker or artist at work in the studio and the firsthand experience of learning. Attentive observation is fundamental to the practice of ethnography, and will always be so. It is also an integral feature of learning. One watches the teacher demonstrate, rehearsing mentally: 'What is he doing there?'; 'How does she do that?' And as learners we also ask ourselves: 'How am I going to manage that?' Such interrogations are valuable exercises for any ethnographer, even if she is not going to attempt to emulate the practitioner. It is one thing to observe *that* something is being done, quite another to comprehend *how* it is being done. As I have just noted, I had watched Chris throwing pots on several visits to his studio, and I had taken photographs of him preparing the clay, throwing and finishing many vessels. As one would expect, it is quite another kind of activity, to try to throw a pot oneself.

I arrived at the studio on the first day of my classes, suitably (shabbily) dressed and carrying old shoes. I knew from previous visits that clay can get everywhere. I was well prepared. Chris began by reminding me that he only ever uses Limoges porcelain, pointing to large plastic-wrapped rolls of it. He also explained that it has to be 'wedged', in order to work out any air pockets or bubbles. He employs 'bull's head wedging', which he demonstrated, kneading and folding the clay in a way that results in the appearance of a pugnacious animal head. I had watched him do it on previous studio visits. De Waal (2015, p. 3) goes on to describe the process:

> I unwrap one and thump it down on to my wedging bench, pull the twisted wire through a third of the way along, pick up the lump and push it into the bench, raising it and pushing it down in a circular motion, like kneading dough. I slow down and the clay becomes a sphere.

Then, after a cup of coffee, Chris sat at the wheel, centred a lump of clay on it and made a cylindrical pot. It is, he explained, the pot he always starts with as it requires control of the clay, rather than him simply allowing it to move outwards under centrifugal force. It calls for more thought and more skill. He quickly transformed the ball of clay in the centre of the wheel into a flat disk, a bit like an English muffin or an ice-hockey puck. He then used the fingers of both hands to create a depression in the centre of the clay, and showed me how he was using a needle to check the thickness of the clay beneath the central depression. Then he used his fingers to draw up the clay. The fingers of his left hand were placed inside the pot, supporting the clay, he explained, while the fingers of his right hand drew the clay up, starting right at the bottom where the bulk of the clay was. The inside finger is not applying any pressure, but providing support, so the fingers of the two hands work together doing different, complementary things. The clay seems to obey him and rises without any visible effort on his part. To an as yet untutored observer like me, it looks as though his hands are following the clay, rather than the reverse. His hands move up and down smoothly in one plane, while the clay revolves on the wheel. Chris pointed out the tools we would be using: the needle, used to check the thickness of the clay, a small sponge and another sponge on a stick. There is water to keep the hands wet. The wheel is, of course, the largest and most prominent of the tools. Together with the rest of the assemblage, it demands precision and coordination.

It was soon my turn to try to emulate what Chris had been doing. Like so many activities of this sort, it engenders nervousness and embarrassment. In some ways, it is silly to feel like that: nobody expects a complete beginner to be anything other than ham-fisted, and there is no audience apart from a teacher who has seen it all before. One thing is self-evident when I come to try throwing my own pots. Unlike my learning experience in the glass studio, there is no guiding hand to 'hold the other end'. At the wheel, with a small ball of clay, I am on my own. Like so many of these novice tasks, the first attempts feel like stepping off the observer's platform of safety into a void of practical incompetence. Without that risky step, however, there is no phenomenological strangeness, and one can lapse too easily into passive watching rather than sensory engagement.

Finding the right position to work at the wheel is important and not perfectly straightforward. In the first, and most trivial, place, I did not find Chris's bicycle-saddle-shaped stool easy to sit on, occasionally being in danger of toppling backwards. Also, because I have short legs, I sometimes found myself reaching uncomfortably for the foot pedal that controls the wheel. Most importantly, getting my arms, hands and fingers in the right place was not easy, and sometimes felt 'unnatural'. I reminded myself that many activities that require manual dexterity, from touch-typing to playing a stringed instrument, or holding a golf club or tennis racquet, involve the hands and the fingers in positions that are not natural, such as arching the wrist. Chris pointed out that I should rest my arms on the edge of the wheel table, and keep a strong shape. It is, however, too easy to relax and let the arms drop, or the wrist to collapse. Indeed, the studio is a setting where the body has to be schooled into new shapes and one has to find a way to relax the limbs and shoulders while keeping them in new, correct orientations.

Chris centred the clay for me for each of the pots we made. On one occasion, he left me to start on my own, and walked away, but although I tried to do exactly as he had in creating a perfectly round disc of clay, I ended up with a poorly formed, uneven lump, and Chris had to rescue it. As I started to work on the clay, I found it relatively easy to create that first central depression, although I had to concentrate on making my arms stable, leaning forward and over the clay, and making sure my fingers were working together. When I didn't keep the fingers under control, little bits of clay crept up between my fingers, creating a lump, like a small nipple, in the middle of the depression. As the day progresses, I get more confident in doing it. I use the needle to gauge the depth of the base, usually finding I am too cautious, so that there is always plenty left when I first check. I cannot judge the likely thickness of the clay by eye or by feel: repeated physical checking is required. Having established the initial depression, the task is to draw the clay outwards into a shape a bit like a wheel hub, or an ashtray. A rimmed disc is the result. Pulling the clay with the fingers to create that shape was *relatively* straightforward.

But drawing up the clay was much more tricky. As Chris had demonstrated, it is about getting the fingers to work together, but doing somewhat different things. I try to apply his advice: the fingers inside the pot are supporting the clay, but not exerting outward pressure, while the fingers on the outside are drawing the clay up. One needs to exert sufficient pressure to move the clay, but avoid squeezing the clay between the inner and outer fingers. If a reminder were needed, it is by no means easy to translate instruction or advice – however simple and straight-forward – into practical action. Getting the right degree of pressure is not easy. In my anxiety not to be too heavy-handed, Chris observed that I was 'caressing' the clay rather than working it upwards. Because Chris makes it look so easy, it does look as if he is just stroking the clay, and it is moving almost of its own accord. And of course that is not the case; there is no magic involved and the clay does not move of its own accord. Sometimes I was being far too tentative, and sometimes I was 'squeezing' the clay, which resulted in uneven walls and some thin sections. Because I was not moving the clay very successfully, some of my pots (such as they were) had heavy bottoms, with too much clay left in the base rather than being drawn into the walls of the vessel. In the case of one pot, I was trying to create a bowl shape, drawing the clay upwards and outwards towards the rim. I found it really difficult not to create uneven ridges in the clay, rather than a smooth progression. On several attempts, I lost the clay completely and the vessel collapsed in on itself. It left an unsightly pile of crumpled clay; the pieces had to be scrapped and the clay added to the spoil heap for recycling. On one occasion, I was just very careless in taking my hands away from the clay while the wheel was still turning, and I knocked the nascent pot with my left arm. Fresh, wet clay moves beautifully when things go well, but is unforgiving when one blunders. As the wheel goes on turning, one cannot simply recover the pot, and a blunder can turn into an unholy mess.

Despite my struggles, we did end the day with a series of seven little pots. They were – unintentionally on my part – of different sizes and shapes, some thicker than others, some bowl-shaped, a couple of others taller. As I finished each one, I slid the wire under the pot to remove it from the wheel, but I asked Chris to lift them off and put them on the surface for me: I was afraid I would crush them in my inexperienced and anxious hands. As we finished off, Chris placed a square of paper over the mouth of each pot, which helps to stabilise them as they dry over-night. With plenty of clay on me, my clothes and shoes, I certainly felt I had had a hands-on experience. And notwithstanding the novice things I have noted, we did at least end the day with a series of pots that we would be able to work on the following day, as Chris introduced me to 'turning'. I left my shabby shoes and jumper in the studio overnight, rather than carrying them back and forth. The shoes were plentifully spattered with clay (oddly satisfying, making me feel like a real craft worker). The pots themselves look surprisingly attractive, arranged on a wooden plank to dry. I take some photographs of them. Quite apart from my own attempts, I really do think that pots are attractive in their 'green' state, before firing and glazing. They have a monochrome simplicity, and the unglazed surface has a pleasing texture in its own right.

Clay: turning

As I have mentioned, the second day was devoted to turning the pots I had made. I had watched Chris turning pots on previous visits to the studio, but I had little idea of what it would involve in practice. It is easy to assume that throwing a pot is the be-all and end-all, but turning is of equal importance, transforming the raw pot into something that is shaped, has a defined rim and a foot. Chris told me that he particularly enjoys turning. It is, he said, a process that reveals the pot that is in the clay. Although the thrown pots (not mine!) can look attractive in their own right, there remains much to be done to transform them into the finished product, ready to be glazed. I look at my efforts from the first day, which have been drying overnight, and with one or two exceptions, I cannot envisage quite how those oddly shaped, lumpish and asymmetrical objects can ever be 'turned' into something presentable. Luckily – and because of Chris's skill – that is not the case, and by the end of the afternoon we have a small collection of objects that look credible. It is an extraordinarily satisfying process, and the results themselves even more so. Turning does indeed turn those ill-formed pots into something presentable.

Having dried somewhat overnight, the clay is no longer so soft. It is like cool leather, with enough strength to hold its shape and to be worked on. The pots can be held in the hand safely, and can be steadied by a hand, or with downward pressure when they are on the wheel during the turning. Chris explains the tools we shall be using today. They are few and simple. They include a number of loop tools, that have small, differently shaped metal loops at each end of a slender wooden handle, kidney-shaped pieces of thin, pliable metal, a little reminiscent of a guitar plectrum, a needle, a sponge and a piece of chamois leather. Chris began by working on a couple of pots while I watched and took some photo-graphs. He picked up some cone-shaped objects and asked me if I knew what they are called. I remembered seeing them in the studio on an earlier visit, but I had to confess I didn't know. They are, he explained, 'chucks', made of raw, unfired clay so they are still able to absorb water and stick to the wheel head, and are used to hold and support a pot on the wheel, if needed. (I didn't ever use one myself, partly because I was nervous about introducing another variable, another potentially moving part into that micro-system on the wheel.)

Chris centred each pot for me, dampening the wheel and pushing the pot firmly in place, rim down. Hardly surprisingly, he was able to work swiftly and confidently. Working on the base, in order to make a foot, he made a circular mark, maintaining a constant distance inside the bottom of the pot, guiding the pin with his finger against the outside of the base.

As the wheel turned, he then used one of the loop tools to take clay out of the base, leaving a rim to form the foot. He started at the centre, holding the tool almost parallel to the base, moving it outwards towards the guide-line, and back towards the centre. The clay came away smoothly, evenly and consistently.

Then Chris worked on the exterior wall of the pot. Using a different looped tool, he worked on removing clay, moving the tool smoothly up and down the pot, and following a curve to define the overall profile of the pot's exterior. He then took a kidney tool and used it to smooth the pot's surface. When he used the looped tool, the clay came away consistently and smoothly, like the peel coming off a skillfully peeled apple. The kidney produced a fine shower of clay particles, but they came away from the clay in an even shower. All the surplus clay gathers in the space around the wheel, from which it can be emptied into the dustbin of waste, ready for recycling.

It then came to my turn to try my hand at turning, working with my own pots. When I was excavating the bases, using the looped tool that Chris chose for me, I had repeated problems. The idea is to keep the head of the tool flat, and to move it from the centre towards the outside and back again. The tool is thus moved back and forth, shaving away clay. But each time I tried it, the tool snagged, and started going round with the rotating pot. It was annoying, although Chris was able to rescue the situation. I described to him what I was doing as 'gouging' the clay. The tool was digging into the clay, getting caught, and thus racing round with the pot, which only made things worse. After several rather frustrating trials, I worked out what was wrong. I was holding the tool between thumb and fingers like a pen or pencil. And therefore I was unconsciously orienting it like a pencil, pointing down at too sharp an angle, probably about 30–40°. I was not trying to follow the pot, but that was a 'natural' movement at times, as opposed to keeping the tool in one plane while the pot itself moved round. I needed to hold it at a much flatter angle, so I pronated my wrist, so that my index finger was on top of the tool, managing to keep its orientation at a much more shallow angle. Although it was by no means perfect, it was better – although even then I still risked digging in a bit, rather than moving the tool smoothly back and forth. It was in itself yet another lesson on the importance of angles.

I found using a different looped tool on the outside of the pot a bit easier, and a lot less frustrating. I was able to cradle the pot with my left hand; that not only steadied the pot, but also seemed to steady me. It brought me closer into the work, and I made a better, more compact shape of my body while working on it. The soft solidity of the cool clay was also reassuring, feeling as it did much less fragile than the wet clay of yesterday. Chris indicated which lines I could follow in shaping the pot. I felt reasonably comfortable moving up and down the side of the pot as it turned on the wheel, and overall it was a more successful action for me than several others. Again, it was always a matter of trying to find the right pressure with the tool. It was easy to be too cautious and conservative – just like my 'caressing' of yesterday. So instead of removing strips of clay smoothly, I quite often found myself irregularly removing small flakes and particles. I came to evaluate my pressure by noting the quality of the removed strips that were coming off the clay, which was variable as my turning was irregular.

Shaping the pots by following a curve was most satisfying. I had to concentrate on getting right into the bottom of the pot or right up to the rim. I also had to concentrate on doing it purposefully, rather than just running the tool's head up and down the exterior of the pot aimlessly. The next stage was working with the kidney-shaped metal tool, concentrating on gripping it firmly and introducing a slight curve in the edge. It wasn't easy to keep an edge in smooth contact with the clay. So again I sometimes found myself going through the motions, passing the kidney over the surface without a clear purpose, so my removal of the clay was uneven at times. But somehow or other I managed. One or two of the pots 'I' had made the previous day had a lot of clay in the base and towards the bottom and I had to take out a good deal of it. I had also managed, quite by accident, to create a waisted pot – a bit of a lopsided hour-glass shape. I quite liked that accident, but with turning, it was possible to transform it into a more conventionally shaped vessel. We also had to deal with the rim of the pots. Some I put a bevelled edge on. It creates a pleasing transition between the inside and the outside, and can also provide a margin between glazes. One or two pots I gave a smoothly rounded rim, finished off with the strip of chamois leather, or with the sponge.

Chris suggested we put a handle on one of yesterday's pots; there was one with straight sides where I seemed to have got the clay fairly high that could become a little mug. 'Are you ready to pull a handle?' he asked. I said certainly I was. So Chris demonstrated. He took some small quantities of clay and rolled several into a carrot-like or bullet-like shape. Then with hands wetted in a plastic jug of warm water, he dunked the carrot; 'This is the point when the twelve-year-olds in the class start sniggering'. Holding the clay in his left hand, pointing vertically down, he used his right hand to draw the clay down, in a 'milking' motion, flattening it somewhat between thumb and index finger so that it became a strap-like strip of clay. When he had done so, he hung the strip from the side of the bench. He did three. Then I tried to copy him, concentrating on pulling the clay down in a smooth motion. I succeeded well enough in creating two strips that Chris hung next to his. Chris then showed me how to put a handle onto a mug, attaching it with a space below the rim, saying he doesn't like the place for the thumb to be right at the top of the handle when holding a mug, and smoothed the clay into the body of the pot, top and bottom. He then used a small roll of clay to fill in the space between the bottom of the handle and the body of the pot. Chris then cut a length from one of my clay strips. He checked what profile of handle I preferred; I said one with an upward curve, not a simple D-shape. So then I copied him in attaching it top and bottom, smoothing the clay out into the wall of the pot, and filling in the gap at the bottom. It looked tolerably convincing.

Chris and I then talked about glazing. I thought it should be classic Chris Keenan – celadon with tenmoku inside, or celadon with a tenmoku 'blob'. But it would be a long while until the pots are glazed and fired – several months. They will have to wait until Chris and Carina have amassed an array of things that need to go in the electric furnace. And so I must contain myself patiently, confining my enthusiasm to photographing my pots, and then posting some of the photos on social media. It is a case of deferred gratification.

Clay: reflecting

Working with clay, especially when throwing, is one of the most intensely tactile of experiences. Unlike several other crafts and tasks, during throwing the contact with the material is unmediated. It is, literally as well as metaphorically, hands-on engagement. One feels the clay directly, its strength or weakness, its thickening and its thinning, its relative moisture and dryness, its cool surface. One can pinch the wall of a pot between one's fingers, and gauge the thickness, and how even or uneven it is (though I was not very good at that). One can feel the weight of the pot, and judge whether that weight is evenly distributed. A weighty, bottom-heavy pot has a very different feel from a pot in which the clay is evenly distributed, even though they are equally heavy. Pots always need to be handled, in their finished state, and during the process of making. Finished pots need to be touched, handled, even cuddled. The curve of a wall can be understood by touch as well as by eye. Indeed, letting one's fingers trace the swell and spring of a well-made pot is a fundamental part of the pleasure to be derived from it. If I lightly run a finger or a hand down a pot in the making, I can try to judge where the surface is uneven, where there is a ridge or a shoulder and where, therefore, turning should remove the clay.

The cool, smooth feel of the porcelain pot that is ready for turning is especially pleasing. 'Leather-hard' it takes a tool, and can be held and supported in the hand. It contrasts with the fragility of the soft wet clay when it is being thrown. The clay on the wheel has its intrinsic integrity, but its form and emerging beauty are easily spoiled. A mistake, a careless movement, can reduce a growing pot to a lump of shapeless clay in an instant. The clay has an organic feel; worked on with warm wet hands, the emerging pot could be something like a baby creature. It is too fanciful, no doubt, to think of that organic thing emerging from the original slimy mud that is clay in terms of something akin to a life-form. But it can feel like that. One holds the pot carefully and caringly, like something newly born.

As I have noted, physical posture is important. I said to Chris that I was conscious in other settings of hunching my shoulders. Carina was in the studio, working on her own pieces. 'Are you breathing?' she called to me from her bench. 'Yes. I try not to hold my breath. But sometimes when I am trying to concentrate, can be hard, remembering to breathe'. Breathing normally is one of the disciplines of the body, together with the right posture and physical relaxation, that novices like me need to learn. Carina teaches, and clearly is familiar with novices' habit of holding their breath. Later I am reminded that breathing is a necessary part of competence for many occupations: not just singers or musicians, but even members of the military (Lande 2007). It is important to let the tool do the work, and to maintain a proper bodily shape, because the tool cannot do the work for us, unless that tool is part of a well-managed body. The tool and the body create a single system. So the tool can only do its work if it is held properly, with the right orientation, and with the right degree of firmness. So when working at the wheel, one needs to maintain a solid base, with one's arms resting on the rim. Using the foot pedal to control the wheel itself adds a further tactile satisfaction, but also an extra degree of complexity. There is nothing intrinsically hard in pressing a pedal to start the wheel turning and to control its speed. But occasionally, when I was trying to concentrate, I know I inadvertently leaned forward over the pot and at the same time pressed down with my foot. The wheel whizzed round ever faster, and I lost control completely, sometimes losing the pot altogether. 'Letting the tool do the work' here also means letting the wheel do the work. I sometimes had to resist the pre-conscious urge to follow the clay round, rather than holding a tool steadily while the clay revolved against it. Throwing and turning are partly about *planes*, just as most craft activities are also about angles. The tool in the hand works vertically or horizontally in a plane that it is tangential to the circular motion of the wheel, and hence of the clay.

The pots, in their glazed and unglazed states, might remind us of the sensory experience of *surfaces*. Glazed ceramics, such as the porcelain pots made by Chris Keenan – and hence those by me – have shiny surface.

They are usually smooth and have hard, reflective surfaces. The unglazed pots have a matt surface that it is, in some ways, more inviting than the finished glazed state. The principles of sensory ethnography, and of applied phenomenology, need to include attention to surfaces. They are both visual and haptic. Touch is important in the making of pots, and also in appreciating them. The same is true of the glassmaking I described in the last chapter. The sheen of glass, clear or coloured, is intrinsic to the appeal of most-blown glass vessels. (Sometimes ground-glass surfaces disrupt the smooth surfaces.) Touch and feel are, or should be, central to a sensory, carnal ethnography.

Paterson (2009) offers a valuable overview of the treatment of haptic knowledge in human geography, and with wider significance beyond that particular discipline. He notes that 'the body' has been granted significance as a topic in a great deal of current social science, but writing *about* sensations of touch and feeling is less common, and is more difficult – not least in terms of finding appropriate language. Consequently, embodied fieldwork is actually rather under-developed. The dominance of the visual endures, Paterson suggests. He echoes Crang (2003) who suggests that there is an absence of work on and from 'haptic knowledges'. While touch has received some degree of attention in recent years (see Classen 2005), there remain need and opportunity to explore further haptic aspects of embodied fieldwork in diverse settings. Craft, and similar activities of practical making, provide ample opportunity to explore the role of touch and surface in everyday objects.

There is, for example, the case of 'sheen'. Douny (2013) writes about Dogon silk textiles, where the sheen of the fabric, especially as it catches the African sun, is prized. As Douny notes, 'Sheen is a visual quality that certain surfaces possess sand that is magnified by virtue of reflecting light. It attracts the "eye" and triggers a reaction of emotion in the viewer. The triad sheen, light and color is embedded into cultural and multisensorial experiences of social, natural and spiritual worlds...' (p. 62). More widely, silky, shiny, polished surfaces can carry connotations of luxury, the quality of 'finish' signifies surfaces of 'quality'. The translucence of glass and the glazed surfaces of ceramics invite more than purely visual appreciation. They also provide tactile surfaces that mean the vessels can be appreciated (or not) through being held, caressed and stroked. Their tactile surface brilliance may also be enhanced by our sense of the vessels' brittle fragility.

There is something intensely gratifying about 'making' a pot – however much it needed rescuing and remedial work by Chris. Turning was surprisingly gratifying. I had assumed – naively – that it would all be in the throwing, and in retrospect had paid insufficient attention to the turning when I had watched Chris do it. Of course, his thrown pots do not need to be rescued the way mine were. But throwing – wet hands on compliant wet clay, the moving wheel – is what appears in popular images of the potter's craft, and craft fairs and the like offer a taste of throwing. I had, if I thought about it at all, assumed that turning was a more humdrum activity, just finishing off the piece, by creating a foot or a rim. But in the event, turning was almost more pleasing than the throwing: not least because my attempts at throwing were pretty poor in comparison. Chris was so right about revealing the pot within – in a way that sculptors have talked about revealing the sculpture that is in the stone, or even releasing it from the stone. In my case, turning was an opportunity to rescue some poorly thrown and ill-formed pots, improving the profile, making the walls more even, taking away excess clay and smoothing the surface. Some of the pots were rescued even further, as Chris could remove upper portions that were especially wonky, so that they could be finished off better: the result was several attractively shaped small, shallow bowls or dishes. When I left the studio at the end of our second day, I was able to photograph a small collection of pots that looked tolerably 'meant'. They had shape, rims and feet. The worst of their irregularities had been smoothed and trimmed away.

My best pots

In thinking about such craftwork, and learning how to make craft objects, it makes sense in many cases to think about 'tools' in a rather restricted way. That is, to think and write primarily about those tools that are hand-held – such as chisels, knives or hammers. In this chapter, and in others in this book, we certainly encounter such tools. The jacks and wooden blocks in the glass studio, the loops and sponges for ceramics, the woodworking implements we shall encounter later. It is easy to invest such hand tools with a special, romantic significance, and it is true that they often provide a material link with the past, and with tradition therefore. But we should not overlook the wider environment of the 'studio'. The studio is itself a rather special place. The worker, the studio, the materials she or he works with are an assemblage, a Gestalt. The maker's body is itself aligned with those physical resources. The potter's body engages with the wheel and the clay simultaneously, in a physical arrangement that demands a certain choreography. The hand and the eye, the tool and the material are all brought together, as is the maker's entire body. The foot engages with the wheel, whether it be a traditional kick-wheel or an electric wheel controlled by a foot-pedal. The maker's embodied work calls for a posture, a physical shape, a structure that facilitates physically efficient work. This is not a static assemblage. There is movement. There is a choreography of the studio, and each craft in each studio calls for its own choreographed movements, its own paths between and across physical space. As Ingold (2013) puts it:

> ...technical intelligence is to be found neither in the brain nor in the hand, nor even in the tool it holds. An object that might be used as a tool is, in and of itself, no more than an inert lump of stone, wood or metal of a certain shape. Likewise...the hand is merely an arrangement of skin, bone and muscle tissue and the brain an immense tangle of neurons. Intelligence belongs to none of these things, taken singly. It rather inheres in the technical act, the gesture, in which they are brought together.

Although I have never been personally committed to working with tools and raw materials, my experience in the ceramics studio was fascinating. It was a brief introduction to something that could become almost obsessive. As I have remarked before, such focused work means that, for its duration, *nothing else matters*. It engages one's total concentration and one's physical commitment. While the imperfections of apprentice-pieces are frustrating, the (distant) prospect of improvement can invite a longer-term engagement with the craft. Edmund de Waal (2015) captures something of this engagement, although in his case, it has a double aspect. Working the clay is an intense experience of being in the moment, but it also connects the maker to a long history of the materials and the craft:

> And I throw the ball of clay into the centre, wet my hands and I am making a jar now and pulling the clay up with the knuckle of my right hand on the outside, three fingers of my left tensed inside to

support, as the walls grow taller like an exhalation, something being said. Because the clay is the present tense and a historical present, I'm here in Tulse Hill, just off the South Circular road in South London, in my studio behind a row of chicken takeaways and a betting shop, sandwiched between some upholsterers and a kitchen-joinery workshop, and as I make this jar I'm in China. Porcelain is China. (p. 4)

The crafts draw us simultaneously into a vivid, concentrated present, and evoke a past, tradition, geography: glass from Venice, porcelain from China.

Clay: postscript

Chris offered to glaze the pots for me, using two glazes – celadon and tenmoku – and to fire them, adding that I would have to wait for the kiln to be used. I said that was fine. I waited, and then temporarily forgot about the pots. Then weeks later they popped back into my mind and I enquired as to their progress. Chris emailed back, saying that they were now ready, attaching a photograph, which I printed off as a black-and-white image. I noted that there were six pots in the picture. The picture I had taken of them grouped together when they were 'green' (before firing or glazing) showed seven. No matter, I would probably find out that one of them had broken in the kiln, as can readily happen to the best of pots. So I arranged to visit Chris in the studio to pick them up.

I arrived, as arranged, in the afternoon. Chris had had other com-mitments earlier in the day. The studio was looking especially neat and tidy, as Chris and Carina were preparing for a visit to the studio by a journalist. They were both there when I arrived and they greeted me warmly. Chris had put my pots out on the otherwise clear and clean bench top. I looked at them. There were still just six. They were (mostly) attractive, but seemed much smaller than I had remembered them under my hand and by eye at the end of the two days. 'Of course, they shrink in the kiln', Chris said, anticipating my response and perhaps disappoint-ment. Of course, I thought, drying all of the moisture out is bound to reduce the porcelain. But they did seem awfully wee. I pointed out to Chris I had come with a suitable bag in which to take away my pots. Chris offered a cup of tea, and the three of us chatted. Carina was composing an email on her laptop, and would be teaching that evening. I really didn't want to hold them up for any length of time. But I said to Chris, 'Did one of my pots fail in the kiln? There were originally seven, but now there's only six'. Chris said, no, nothing had smashed. I said it really wasn't important, though as far as I could see it was one of my nicest ones that had gone missing. However, Chris looked on the shelves where he stacks his own work, and, to my relief, he found my missing one. It looked pretty. Carina held it and weighed it in her hand, and turned it over. 'It has a good rim', she said, 'And a good foot'. 'Thank you', I replied, 'It was my best rim'. This form of member-validation made me feel pretty special (although I enacted due modesty, I hope). But it was a great relief, as my own photograph had suggested that the little pot was indeed my 'best one'. Chris had implied a certain scepticism, when I first raised the issue. 'I've got photographic evidence', I said (in a joking tone), showing him on my phone. 'Perhaps there's also the secret tapes', he suggested. The little pots looked pleasing in the studio. As soon as I got them home, I unpacked them eagerly and took a really good look at them. My instinct and Carina's judgements were sound. The pot that nearly got away had the most pleasing shape, rim and foot. Unlike several of the others, it was not too heavy, and felt like a piece of porcelain should. On close inspection, at least two of the others were still lumpish and clumsy despite the turning. One felt much heavier than such a small porcelain pot should, as it still had too much clay in it. One of the others was far from symmetrical.

5

Two Spoons: Wood and Silver

Materials

We have already encountered clay and glass studios that furnish examples of materials, tools and fire. In this chapter, I shall develop those themes further, focusing on work with wood and silver. Once more, these exemplars are derived from short classes with expert craftworkers. In the case of wood, I took a one-day class with Nic Webb, who was then working in Vanguard Court, South London, in a studio very close to Chris Keenan's, and Chris had recommended him to me. It was one of Nic's regular classes, which I shared with two young women learners. I spent two separate days working with Eleanor (Ellie) Swinhoe, who makes jewellery in her home in Frome, Somerset. I had met her at a craft fair in Cardiff and had sought permission to take a class with her. She regularly provides introductory courses. The silversmithing, conducted over two separate days, was one-to-one tuition with Ellie (and Barley the cat). It is in the spirit of all of the substantive elements of this book that the various processes are recounted in concrete detail.

Wood and silver both brought me into direct, haptic contact with physical materials. They were, at a personal level, reminders of how ill at ease I always have been with things like wood and metal; I feel no affinity with them. Consequently there is no difficulty in treating the tasks of working with them as 'anthropologically strange'. If anything, the reverse is true, as my reluctance and aversion readily create the necessary alienation effect. But here we come very directly in touch (literally) with materials and materiality. Equally, in both settings, we encounter tools yet again. Tools of course have their own materiality, while our engagement with our 'raw' materials (wood and metal) is mediated by tools as well as coming more directly through the bare hands. Both the woodworking and the silversmithing called for a practical understanding of tool use. As we shall see in the first example, the woodworking is almost completely dependent on the appropriate use of the right tools. And that in turn implies techniques of the body. Posture and control are as important as the raw materials or the tools in the making. In these studios, the ethnographer is particularly free to focus on 'things' and their 'thingness'. Here, as in similar milieux, the ethnographer is absorbed in the moment, and in the task at hand. For that moment, nothing beyond the studio can *matter*. Focus is fixed on the materials and on the physical engagement with the object-in-the-making. In addressing these issues, I find myself substantially in agreement with Ingold (2011), when he argues that in studies of materials, there is too much emphasis on 'materiality', and not enough on 'materials': 'in this regard, it is significant that studies of so-called material culture have focused overwhelmingly on processes of consumption rather than production....' (p. 26). In his own treatment, Ingold provides a careful, reflective account of sawing a wooden plank. The steps in sawing

> ....do not follow one another in succession, like beads on a string. Their order is processional, rather than successional. In walking, every step is a development of the one before and a preparation for the one following. The same is true of every stroke of the saw. Like going for a walk, sawing a plank has the character of a journey that proceeds from place to place, through a movement that – though rhythmic and repetitive – is never strictly monotonous'. (p. 53)

Working with wood and metal gave me ample opportunity to experience such rhythmic repetition and its 'processional' nature.

A concern with the materials to hand is certainly not apparent everywhere. Woodward's textbook on 'material methods', for instance, has remarkably little to say about actual, concrete engagements with material objects (Woodward 2020). Woodward says of ethnographic methods: '... given that you are physically present with people in situ, it is impossible not to smell, feel, move with and see people and things around you .... Immersion is by definition multi-sensory' (p. 120). In practice, however, Woodward's accounts of methods are disproportionately devoted to interviews rather than participation, and to visual rather than embodied practical methods. I mention this not in order to be negative about Woodward's work, but to acknowledge that it is a fair reflection of the current state of play. Even in an intellectual context where 'ethnographic' work is celebrated, an emphasis on talk (via interviews) rather than participation is pervasive. Likewise, 'sensory' methods too often seem to result in visual methods (photographs or video recordings) rather than thoroughly embodied engagements and practical learning.

The wooden spoon

There were three of us learners for Nic's day class. As we arrived in his studio in the morning, Nic had already trimmed some branches of lime, which, being soft, would be easy for us to work with. He had also selected some cherry wood, which is harder, but, he said, rewarding to work with, and we might like to try it (I never did, as the one spoon called for all my time and concentration.) He put the pieces of lime on the floor between us and invited us each to pick out a piece of wood. I chose a piece that I told Nic I was 'bonding with'. I felt that I was taking the easy way out, as the piece I chose looked very simple – no knots or irregularities, and with a straight grain. As the day went on, I was partly pleased that I had such a simple piece of wood to work with, but I also regretted it, because my resulting spoon seemed bland, being very plain, in pale lime, with no grain or distinctive characteristics. My piece had bark on one side, and was fairly uniform in width and thickness, being rather narrow. This would constrain the size of the bowl I could make for my spoon. As things worked out, my own spoon was in every way thin, pale and tentative.

Once we had each chosen a piece of wood, we moved on to the next stage. Nic explained that we needed to keep an inch or so at the end of our wood, to give us something to grip while we worked. This is especially necessary, as we are moving on to work with an axe. To a complete novice like me, it seems rather counter-intuitive to use an axe for something as delicate as a decorative spoon. But as Nic began to demonstrate, we started to see how the axe helps to shape the spoon. They were, he explained, perfectly ordinary axes, though obviously well maintained and properly sharpened. I would normally think of an axe in terms of hefty swipes, the tool held firmly at the end of the handle and wielded quite vigorously, and that is just what Nic acknowledged, stressing that it is not used to 'bludgeon' the wood. Instead, he demonstrated holding the axe with a finger on the back of the blade itself, the axe held in a sort of pistol grip. Then he showed how to use the axe to chip into the wood to make a small start, and then to tap the wood on the floor, rather than wielding the axe. The wood is banged at a slight angle, on the corner diagonally opposite from the position of the axe. In Nic's hands, the axe produced the neatest possible starting points, and as he brought the wood down, he let the weight of the axe do the work. Slivers of wood came away easily. Like everything Nic demonstrated, the relationship between hand, tool and wood seemed perfectly harmonious, so that even such a relatively large object as an axe could be made to perform precise work on the wood, while the wood itself seemed perfectly obedient – coming away along the grain just as it should.

Following Nic's instructions, we each mark out the bowl of our spoon. We need to describe a circle or an oval with a pencil, making a mark a few millimetres in from the edge of the wood itself. This is the line we shall work to. Nic uses a coin to create the rounded end of his spoon shape. His pencil drawing is clear and confident; he runs the pencil round, using a finger to guide him and to keep a firm line a little way in from the end of the wood. Mine is not. Even in just drawing the outline of a wooden spoon–bowl, my effort looks uncertain and amateurish. The line is ragged, and the shape asymmetrical. Hardly surprisingly, my own use of the axe is not quite the same as Nic's. He made a small opening mark with the axe, and then as he tapped the spoon at a slight angle, wood came away. I do not seem even to make that clean, confident mark to start each movement. I take several chips at the wood, almost always coming down at a different spot. And then, having got the axe head into some sort of starting position, I think I am holding the wood at too great an angle. The consequence is that the axe does not perform the long cuts that Nic has demonstrated, removing substantial amounts of wood along its length. Rather, I seem to be chipping away small nibbles of wood, and the axe is slipping. The process is removing wood, but not efficiently or effectively, and certainly it lacks Nic's apparently effortless shaping. I am kneeling, working on the studio floor, and after a little while, I realise that bits of me are aching. My lower back in particular is giving me discomfort: it is never good when it comes to stooping and bending, and kneeling is not an accustomed posture. Likewise, my hands are starting to ache because I am gripping things too tightly. My left hand is getting sore from gripping the end of the wood, and despite my best intentions, I am gripping the axe too anxiously. I get up to move a bit to stretch my back, and my thighs are feeling the effects of kneeling. This is not quite the 'processional', rhythmic performance that Nic had been demonstrating.

My piece of wood has the semblance of shape: the bowl end is still plain and solid, and it still has an extra inch or so of wood, where I am gripping it. It has the shape of a sort of thick spatula, with a longish 'handle', rudimentary shoulders and a plain block at the end. The shoulders still lack definition, however, and I point this out to Nic, who is moving between us, checking on progress. He helps me out with a few effective passes with the axe. As I go on chipping, the thing continues to develop shape. Now I have a handle, which has a fairly flat top surface, but an asymmetrical, ridged back. The next stage of the spoon involves working with a knife, which has an elegant simplicity of its own, with a curved blade and a wooden handle. It is, Nic assures us, extremely sharp, demonstrating by making cuts through a sheet of paper. He takes great care to show us exactly how to hold the knife and how to cut with it. There are two cutting motions with the knife, and two grips. First Nic demonstrates how *not* to do it. Cutting as one might sharpen a pencil can result in an uncontrolled action and likely to result in accidents, and cutting towards the hand holding the spoon is likely to end in a cut to the thumb. So, first we can hold the knife with the finger and thumb on or behind the blade, so that we are gripping it near where blade and handle meet. We cut towards us, holding the end of the spoon well away from us in our left hand. This is done on our lap. Nic demonstrates: he is sitting with his knees together, making a firm lap, his elbows tucked in. His is a compact, controlled posture. He shows how it makes a solid base for us to work. Because I only have short legs, I need a piece of wood under my feet to create the right sort of working lap.

The second way of using the knife is to cut away from us. The grip is different: the forward pressure comes from the thumb of the left hand, which overlaps the right. This again produces a controlled action. The only pressure comes from the left-hand thumb: Nic shows us that when he is doing it the nail of his thumb (the right, of course) is white – showing that the forward pressure is going through it. Given the sharpness of the knife, this technique is very important: it gives control in the cutting, and therefore ensures safety as well.

I can now do more with my spoon. Nic shows us to draw a further pencil line to define the thickness of the handle. Again, he is adept at running a pencil along the line of the wood, keeping the line firm and maintaining a consistent thickness of wood. Again, my line is scruffy and uncertain. I try to cut the way that Nic has demonstrated. I find it difficult to maintain his well-balanced posture. He seems to be able to cradle the spoon in his grasp and to make small, controlled movements. My movements are small enough, perhaps, but nowhere near as effective. And I certainly find it hard to establish the stable lap and arms that Nic manages. I cut in both directions. The sharpness of the knife is satisfying. It allows me to cut away wood and to carve the spoon more or less as I intend. I concentrate on reducing the handle of the spoon, and improving the definition of the transition between the handle and the bowl. I avoid cutting myself. I am careful with the blade of the knife, but I realise that I am at my least vigilant during the transition between one action and another, or when turning the spoon round. I focus on the spoon rather than the blade at such times. Moreover, when my hand starts to get a bit tired, not only are my actions more sloppy, but I slip into careless jabbing, and my grip relaxes into a more dangerous shape. At one point Nic calls over, 'Is that thumb in control, Paul?' I have to acknowledge that it isn't.

To this point my 'spoon' still had a square end – the end where I gripped it, and where the bowl would eventually be formed. The time came for this to be trimmed. The last inch – the bit beyond the bowl – had to be taken off, and Nic did that for me with a saw, which he also used to remove the corners, so that the end of the wood now had a roughly oval or pointed shape to it. I used the knife to start shaping the bowl. Nic had told us to identify the centre of the bowl on both sides of the wood, and to use that centre to define a line on the underside, so that one would reduce the wood away from that line. The centre would then remain at the deepest point of the spoon's bowl. I try to carve away wood from the underside of the bowl. But I always seem to leave lumps and bumps. I seem also to have created a couple of flat spots. Rounding them off leaves me in danger of cutting away so much wood that I might flatten the thing out too much, leaving virtually no wood for a bowl at all. A compromise on my part: a bowl that is a little bit lumpy, and an end to cutting.

So now we have reached the point where we have a tolerably well-defined handle and a flattened knob at one end. Turning the solid knob into a bowl will be the next main aspect of making the spoon. It will involve the use of a new tool. Nic demonstrates again. We have to use a chisel with a curved blade. The most important thing is that in essence the hand holding the chisel remains still, while the other hand turns the wood. The use of the chisel is this: one takes small scoops of wood (like using an ice-cream scoop, I suggest to Nic); the chisel is used at right angles to the grain of the wood (quite unlike the previous tools); it is a matter of turning rather than gouging or digging; a series of small cuts. We work our way round the shape of the bowl, 'favouring' the pencil-line, as Nic put it. I realise as I make a start that I am not being consistently accurate: at times I seem to have strayed a bit too close to my line. If I am not careful, the wall of the spoon's bowl will be too thin, or uneven, or both.

I say to Nic that I am having difficulty turning the corner inside my spoon. As he had explained to us, and as I had already discovered, there is an easier side and a trickier side to the spoon: it is a matter of one's hands and their relation to the spoon itself. As we carefully remove wood with the chisel, we start from the pencil-line inside the rim of the spoon, so as we go round, we are left with a ridge down the middle of it, where our chisel marks all meet. I try to remove it, but it is not quite as easy as it looks. I point this out to Nic. In particular, I have created a small area where the grain has lifted a bit, and there is a danger of pulling it so that it tears the wood. Nic comes over and does it for me. As usual, it is instructive to see how he can retrieve the situation with a few deft movements with the tool. This sort of repair work is vital to the pedagogy, and also to the completion of the task in hand. Nic provides a helping hand to each of his learners in turn, rescuing and repairing.

By now my spoon has taken shape. I am not unhappy with it, but it lacks character. I had intended it to have a flat top surface and a somewhat more 'rustic', 'worked' surface underneath. (To some extent making a virtue out of the accidents of its making.) In the event, the top is not especially flat, and the underside more uneven than interestingly worked. However, it has reached the stage where it needs to be smoothed off. Nic gives me a small sheet of sandpaper, and I set to work rubbing it down. Nic then says to make a 'pebble' with the sandpaper to finish the inside of the bowl. Because the lime-wood is soft, the sandpaper has immediate effect. I smooth off the inside, and the marks left by the tools start to disappear. Nic asks me if I want the end of the handle to be rounded or square. I say 'square' (don't know exactly why), so he takes it over to the bench and saws it off neatly. I sand it a little.

My wooden spoon

My spoon actually resembles a very rough version of something that could be bought cheaply for use in the kitchen. But, as I reminded myself, the exercise is about the processes of learning, and learning the processes of making. In particular, this lesson of the studio is about the materiality of the wood, the tools and the body. It is about letting the tool do the work. Each tool is the embodiment of a long process of development and evolution. The knives and the chisels are perfectly adapted to perform specific kinds of task, to make certain kinds of action possible. Their weight, shape and sharpness are perfectly suited to those tasks. If used appropriately, then the tools make each stage in the making process a controlled one. But such use requires disciplined use. Tools must be held correctly. That is not just a matter of safety, significant though that is. The relationship between the tool, the body (not just the hand) and the wood has to be controlled. Hence the arrangement of the body itself is fundamentally important. Aching hands do not just reflect unaccustomed use, although all new activities find out little muscles that are not normally used in a sustained fashion. My aching thighs remind me that I do not normally kneel for any length of time; they also reflect the importance of embodied technique. Simply put, we novices have a habit of simply gripping things too tightly, and hunching over the work. The whole body is implicated. As I have described, Nic creates a compact shape for his working body: lap, arms, hands. They are managed in such a way as to create a stable working unit. But for the learner, it is easy to lose control. While I can see how Nic controls his movements, copying them is not easy, and it is even harder to maintain such control. I start with my knees and elbows tucked in to define a working space, but as I try to do the work, and as I find things tricky, I lose my shape. I grip the tool wrongly, and my arms and hands are no longer managed properly. My elbows stick out; my fingers migrate on the knife (although I do avoid having an accident).

For the novice, the relationship between intention and execution is problematic. I think I can envisage how I want my spoon to be and to look, and I try to let it follow the width, the curve and the line of the wood. But achieving that intention is hard in the absence of reliable technique. My actions are too tentative, and they are not reliably replicated. I do not remove wood in consistent ways, and because I cannot do so, the piece becomes asymmetrical and uneven. My spoon's handle does not have an elegant curve, and has more of a twist in it than I would like. This is not just a matter of complaint or rueful confession of my own inadequacy. There is a very positive side to this. As I have encountered, and documented from elsewhere – such as glassblowing – the pedagogy is remarkably successful. After all, the day has seen my lump of wood transformed into something that is recognisably a spoon. I haven't damaged myself, and I have coped with a series of tools. Pedagogy is remarkably stable and remarkably effective in such a setting. This in turn reflects something important about craft itself. Materials, tools and techniques embody not just distinctive styles, but also robust ways of working. Ways of working in turn shape ways of instruction: the way of the tool, the way of the body. The material itself, of course, has its own affordances. The lime-wood we have been using has its own degree of softness and its own grain. Other woods have their own characteristics. Each creates productive possibilities, each imposes its own constraints.

Here, therefore, we have an example – or perhaps a series of examples – about learned *technique*. Technique directly links learned action with material resources and artefacts. Technique provides solutions to practical problems. It is simultaneously social and cultural – learned and repeated activities that predictably yield controlled outcomes. Technique also links the practical with the aesthetic. It is embodied in the maker's own bodily actions, and it is embodied in the tools of the trade. The techniques of the body are of fundamental importance, but they are not the whole story, because the body can only act on the materials to hand, and can only work with their inherent possibilities. Those possibilities themselves have to be learned and explored in enculturated, disciplined ways. The pedagogy is stable because the materials and the techniques themselves have a degree of stability. The 'wooden spoon' is proverbially the booby prize, the mocking prize for coming last. In my case, it is quite the reverse. It is a proud achievement. It is a concrete manifestation of the fact that I have learned and done *something*.

The ring and the spoon

I spent two separate days at Ellie Swinhoe's studio in her house. On my first visit, I learned how to make a silver ring, and on the second we made a small silver spoon together. I shall not summarise everything twice, but I again focus on my engagement with the materiality of the metal, of the studio and of the tools I used. Ellie gives me a quick guided tour of the room and introduces what we are going to do. She explains that we are going to start working with copper, as it is much softer than silver and easier to work. She explains that it first needs to be annealed to make it workable. So we go over to the table at the end of the studio. There are several heat-resistant ceramic tiles, and three burners hanging by one's right hand. I am reminded that the bit I really disliked about metalwork at school was the element of fire. I remind myself that really all I need to do is to concentrate. Ellie arranges a small length of copper and explains that the heat of the flame is at the tip of its internal cone. She shows me how to direct the flame round the copper wire and then to heat it from one end, until it starts to change colour, and then to move the heat along its length. Once I have done so, she picks up the copper in a pair of tweezers and dunks it in a bowl of cold water, producing a tiny hiss. It can now be picked up in the fingers and dropped into the pickle pot. Ellie has explained that the pickle pot contains a light caustic solution which cleans the metal.

The metal can then be removed from the pickle pot with a pair of tongs, rinsed and dried on a cloth. It can now be shaped into a ring. This is done at the mandrel, a tapering steel column at a free-standing workstation. Its tapering corresponds to the different sizes of ring, marked in a series of grooves. Ellie puts her strip of copper on the mandrel and deftly shapes it towards a ring, with downwardly angled taps with a rawhide mallet. The copper seems entirely obedient, and forms itself into a circle, its two ends overlapping. Ellie examines the circle and gives it a few taps on each side to ensure that the ring is symmetrically flat. We then go to the jeweller's bench, where Ellie explains that we shall need to saw through the two ends of the ring in a single cut, so that the ends will make a perfect join. She sits herself down, and takes a fretsaw with a very thin blade. Holding the ring firmly with the thumb and forefinger of her left hand, she saws in an upright motion, into the end of one of the v-shaped grooves sawn into the wooden bench peg. This is the central part of the jeweller's bench. It is a removable wooden wedge, mounted onto a fixed metal holder. It is one of the most obviously customised or socialised of tools. It is grooved with three v-shaped cuts that Ellie has made herself. Because she does a lot of drilling there, it is also pock-marked with holes, making it look as if it is infested with woodworm. She saws steadily and confidently, and the two ends fall away, leaving a perfectly clean cut. Then it is back to the other end of the studio, to solder the two ends together. Ellie opens a small plastic container of tiny pieces of solder ('pallions') that look a little like Christmas glitter. She brushes some flux onto the joint, and explains that if the joint is placed over the solder, on a ceramic tile, and then heated, the solder will 'jump' when it reaches the right temperature. Ellie carefully positions the pallions and the ring, and then applies the heat. I confess that although I was peering closely, I couldn't really spot the crucial moment when the solder actually jumped. The ring dunked and retrieved from the pickle pot, Ellie then shows me how to use files and then abrasive paper to clean up the solder area and to polish the ring. Finally, she uses the buffing machine, which has two rapidly revolving brushes, to apply a final polish. She explains that one has to keep a strong grip on the piece and push it firmly into the brush. If one does not keep a firm grip, it can fly out of the fingers.

It is now time for me to try to emulate what Ellie has done, still in copper. She cuts me a length, and we take it over for annealing. I position the copper strip, and cautiously turn on the flame. I remember to apply heat round the copper strip and then to start heating it from one end. I try to ensure that the heat is applied at the inner cone of the flame. Although it is easy to see the metal change colour, I do not have any feel for how long it should be heated, but I seem to get it more or less right, moving the heat fairly evenly along the strip of the metal. Being careful to do things safely, I turn off the burner, carefully pick up the copper strip in the tweezers and pop into the cold water. I remind myself aloud to do this. I feel it is too easy unthinkingly to reach out and pick things up in the fingers.

After dunking the copper strip into the pickle-pot, I need to start shaping my ring on the mandrel. I try to copy Ellie's mallet taps, giving the copper two or three taps a time, angling downwards, at a tangent to the curve of the mandrel. I am pleased to find that the copper is bending itself into a circle, and Ellie makes an approving sound. I am immensely pleased with myself. I realise, however, that there is one issue I need to concentrate on: it would be awfully easy to let the metal slide towards the thinnest end of the mandrel, and hence bending the metal into impossibly small, tight circles. However, I succeed in making a circle of metal that is more or less the right size for my own finger. Self-satisfaction is short-lived. Now I have to saw through the two ends of the ring to make a perfect join. The ring needs to be held very firmly with the finger and thumb of my left hand while I saw with the right. I do not seem to be getting it right, however. First, holding the ring perfectly still with my weak and unaccustomed fingers is harder than it really ought to be, while my sawing just isn't as smooth and regular as it should be, and certainly nothing like Ellie's. I realise I have no idea how my cut is progressing. All I know is that there is no proper alignment of my cutting. I ask Ellie for help. In the first place, she points out, I have the ring too far away, and so I am cutting into the wood rather than through the metal (why couldn't I feel that I wonder). Secondly, the ring has slipped – my grip was indeed poor – and so I have been making a double cut. In the event, I carry on and complete the second cut all the way through the two sections of copper and the ends fall away. Surprisingly, the ends left by my second cut marry up adequately. Trying to keep the saw blade in a vertical plane, and sawing with a steady, regular motion is not easy. At times it sticks and I am conscious of the blade twisting. I say to Ellie that I am afraid of damaging her blade. She replies reassuringly that she has plenty of spare blades.

So, it is time to solder the ring. I apply the flux, conscious that I don't know how much to apply or just how precise I need to be. I dab a bit on round the joint. Then I have to pick up a pallion and place it and the ring on the ceramic tiles. As urged by Ellie, I try to apply heat evenly round the ring to begin with, rather than just at the joint to be soldered. I confess that, again, I could not really see with any certainty when the solder had been taken up. However, it seemed to be OK, so again it was quenched in the cold water, popped in the pickle pot and taken over to the bench to be cleaned up. I worked round the ring, inside and out, with a file. I tried to make sure I was using the file in the same direction, following the curve of the metal, avoiding creating a flat spot. I wasn't sure I could actually see precisely what needed cleaning up, so my filing, and then papering, was perhaps ritualised rather than being purposeful. I then had a go at polishing the piece on the buffing wheel. I was glad I had put on safety goggles, as – rather as Ellie herself had warned – I lost concentration, relaxed my grip on the ring and let it fly out of my fingers. Luckily it did not disappear under anything or between floorboards, and I was able to retrieve it, feeling a bit ashamed of such an elementary blunder. I also learned that one has to push the ring quite firmly into the brush, keeping it moving all the time. One's finger ends can get quite a going-over at the same time.

My copper ring is completed. It looks perfectly plausible. Working with the soft, warm-coloured copper seemed redolent of ancient metal-working, and I thought of Wayland the Smith as a mythological proto-type. It is now time to reproduce the steps in the process to make my silver ring. Ellie cuts a section of silver wire, therefore. This will be a thin ring, not a band – which would presumably take greater skill and management, as well as more precious metal. We take it across the studio to anneal it. Ellie points out that the silver will change colour again, but the colour itself will be different – pink this time. Again, I try to apply the heat evenly round the silver, and then to start heating it from one end; it does indeed go pink. I heat along the short length of the metal. I realise that I need to heat it 'just enough', and do not need to over-do it. I talk myself through picking the hot metal up on tweezers once more, before quenching it and transferring it to the pickle pot. I seem to have the hang of shaping the metal on the mandrel, once more trying to emulate Ellie's angled tapping, keeping the metal moving so that the ring shape is formed. Some light taps also ensure that it is flat.

Having created my ring shape, I then saw through the two overlapping ends. The silver is, of course, less soft than the copper (though soft enough in absolute terms). This time I am more careful to keep the ring firmly pressed down while I saw through. The silver is more resistant than the copper was. I realise that there is considerable pressure on just the finger and thumb. This time, I manage to cut through the two thicknesses without any slippage, and the two ends marry up well and so can be soldered together. I manage to saw fairly evenly and regularly, keeping the blade moving in a vertical orientation. I apply the flux, select a pallion and place the ring carefully over it. The solder flows into the joint, but I still cannot pretend to have observed it properly through the flame. After the pickle pot, I work over the ring with a file in order to tidy it up and use the paper and the buffing machine. Ellie suggests that we might texture the surface of the ring rather than leaving it smooth. So back at the mandrel, I tap the ring gently all over with a round-headed hammer. Ellie has started this for me; her light taps are precise, mine are all over the place, and there is no danger of the decoration being anything other than random. In the end, I am quite satisfied with my ring. It is exactly the right size for my ring finger, which is the size I have been aiming at, although I do not ever envisage actually wearing such a narrow band. It is indubitably evenly round, regular and shiny.

What sort of things have I learned? I have learned yet again how apparently stable such craft pedagogy can be. The equipment, the techniques, the bench – these are all common across studios and prac-titioners, and stable across time. As a consequence, such pedagogy can be extraordinarily successful. An experienced craftworker can take a complete novice like me and take him or her through the same basic techniques with a predictable outcome. At every stage in the process, despite my lack of facility with my hands and with tools, I can feel relatively in control. Getting the angles right is important in this context. I have to try to emulate Ellie in striking on the mandrel at the right sort of angle in order to bend the metal. I need to keep the saw aligned at the right angle to keep it moving smoothly and accurately. This is a craft of precision. This sort of work is on a small scale, and there are fewer degrees of latitude than, say, making my wooden spoon: in the latter case, if the wood splits off unpredictably, then (within limits) I can change the shape of the spoon. As with other practical activities, there are recurrent issues of 'how' and 'when'. I know the metal needs to be heated to make it workable – but how much, for how long, I do not know. Likewise, I am not really sure when the solder has flowed into the joint, and consequently how much longer I need to apply the heat. Like many makers I have met, Ellie conveys a great sense of calm, not least because she has the confidence in all the things where I lack it. The actions that, for me, are clumsy are assured and habituated for her. But unlike my trying to learn from a book or instruction manual, she can see what is 'enough' and guide me appropriately, as well as offering general encouragement and advice. My silver ring is definitely another trophy, and it fits my ring finger perfectly. The measure of success lies in the work and knowledge that went into making it rather than the object itself. I am nonetheless gratified that the ring is as it was intended: round, shiny, the right size.

The silver spoon

My second day, some weeks after making the ring, was devoted to making a silver spoon – a slightly more ambitious and substantial piece than my ring. Safely arrived at Ellie's home, and after sociable conversation, I follow her up to the top-floor studio, precariously balancing a mug of coffee and my camera up the very steep stairs. The studio is, of course, familiar territory by now and I feel comfortable. Ellie has obviously put thought into how the spoon lesson is to proceed, and has made two test pieces in copper, which she shows me. Thinking through the potential structure of the pedagogy is itself a practical, embodied activity for her. The copper spoons in a sense inscribe what might in other contexts be thought of as a 'lesson plan'. The insides of the bowls have an embossed pattern; the outsides are smooth. The handle wraps part-way underneath the bowl. One handle ends in a small circle, the other is plain.

Ellie explains how the embossed pattern is achieved, saying it will introduce me to a piece of equipment we had not used last time – the rolling mill. The pattern is embossed by placing something between two sheets of metal and pressing the sandwich in the rolling mill – which consists of a pair of metal rollers, a large screw on the top used to vary the pressure and a large handle to turn the rollers. Ellie says that she has used a variety of things to produce embossed patterns, including feathers, leaves, coiled wire and even lace. She has also tried using small foil stars used for decorations. We agree to use the stars, which she has already embossed on the copper trial pieces, and which produce a pleasing overall texture.

So in the usual way, we are going to start with copper by way of practise. First a small sheet of copper needs to be annealed. This bit I can remember, making sure to be careful with the flame. Ellie reminds me that the hottest part of the flame is at the tip of the internal cone, where the blue flame is visible. This is one of the very few remaining memories of secondary school science – the Bunsen burner (Delamont, Beynon and Atkinson 1988). We place the copper on the ceramic tiles and I do what I think I have remembered – heating round the object a bit before focusing the heat on the piece of copper. It starts to turn colour quite quickly, and Ellie tells me to stop. I remember to pick it up with tweezers and dunk it in the bowl of cold water to the right hand side. It can now be handled, and I put it into the pickle pot. This routine is, if not exactly habitual, certainly well ingrained. I fish the copper back out, rinse it under the tap and dry it on a cloth. Next it needs to be beaten with the leather mallet, just to ensure that it is flat. Then Ellie sandwiches some stars between our piece and another piece of copper and puts it through the rolling mill. The latter is a bit like a miniature version of the mangles used by my mother and grandmother on laundry days. Ellie says it is a matter of getting the pressure 'just enough', and it's a matter of feel. The rollers need to be set at the right pressure to emboss the pattern. As she adjusts the top screw and pulls on the handle, I can see that a certain amount of physical force is required to overcome the pressure. Ellie performs it all herself. As the copper emerges and is separated from the second layer, there indeed is an embossed pattern of stars.

Now we need to produce a disc from the embossed copper. Ellie takes a jeweller's loupe and scribes round it to create the circular shape we need. She then sits me at the bench once more to saw round the inscribed line. She reminds me that I need to make sure I hold the metal still, to use the grooves in the wooden pin to do the sawing, and to keep the saw vertical. She makes the first cut to start me off, and then lets me get on with it. Sawing the metal really finds out my physical failings. In the first place, I do not seem to have enough physical strength in my left hand to keep the copper firmly in place. It moves a bit, and consequently the saw sticks. I also don't seem to be all that adept at using the saw. Although I try, I don't seem to be using the whole length of the blade, as Ellie has shown me, and one way and other I am not very good at following the circular line. First my cut starts to veer off at a tangent, and then to deflect equally sharply back towards the line. For the first time in my two visits, I am getting hot under the collar and frustrated with myself. I am red with annoyance and embarrassment. Ellie says not to worry. She says that when she first started her training, she had to cut out her initials, and after hours of work, her hands were cramping up. She shows me again how she holds the metal in place. She has strong fingers. Mine are little and feeble. I say to her that my small hands are better suited to writing than to this. Ellie suggests that I finish where I am (about half way round) and cut off the scrap. Deftly she repairs my shoddy workmanship and finishes cutting out the disc.

We then start to shape the bowl. Ellie has a steel block with round hollows of various sizes. She selects the one that best fits the spoon's disc. She then chooses one from a range of domed steel implements, of graduated sizes. She puts a pad of kitchen paper on top of our copper disc, in order to prevent damage to the embossing. I then hit the steel punch with an ordinary hammer. We stop a couple of times to check on progress. The hammering has not been perfectly centred or even, so the bowl, which is slowly taking shape, is a bit lopsided. Ellie replaces it at a slight angle and repeats the process, making the bowl a little deeper and also more symmetrical. We then return to the bench, where I use a large file to try to remove any uneven parts on the rim of the little bowl. Ellie reminds me to use the file in one direction only. She demonstrates, making strong, confident strokes. I try to emulate her, but in truth it remains a poor effort. However, we have a copper bowl for a spoon, and we agree that it is not necessary to go on to make the complete practice spoon.

We proceed to working with silver. Obviously I have not actually become proficient in all of the skills required. And in many ways, I have to confess that I cannot really claim to have made the silver spoon myself. Ellie did most of the skilled work while I did bits of the work. At best it is a collaboration. But then I am already reminding myself that the purpose of today's exercise is ultimately to write about the craft and the learning process, not to make masterworks of my own. So after we have annealed a piece of silver, we emboss it, as we did the copper. This time I try feeding the silver and the copper sheet that sandwich our decorative stars into the rolling mill myself. I understand how adjusting the space between the rollers is largely a matter of feel. I am relieved that I have enough strength to heave on the handle and roll the metal through. It comes out with the embossed pattern clearly visible. Ellie and I agree that we shall get on faster if she saws out the disc herself. In the ideal world, perhaps, I should spend time developing the ability to saw metal efficiently and accurately. But time is short and I am not actually serving an apprenticeship. Ellie, of course, cuts out the circle of silver very smoothly, doing all the things I know I *should* do. It is a mundane activity at this level, although there are obviously other occasions when accurate and detailed cutting would be required. Nonetheless, it illustrates the strangeness of craft hand-work for someone like me.

We form the silver disc into a small bowl in exactly the same way as we did with the copper. I wield the hammer. The bowl starts to take shape, but a little unevenly, so Ellie repositions it carefully and hammers a little more so that the shape is symmetrical. Once more I return to the bench, and use the large file to smooth the rim. As I do so, I realise that I cannot really 'see' what effect I am having, and whether I am filing enough or too much. Silver dust is certainly coming off, but again I really need Ellie to check and complete the process. Now we need to make the spoon's handle. Ellie selects some silver wire, choosing the gauge she thinks we shall need, and clipping off a length from a coil she selects from a cabinet drawer. She herself starts to hammer it in order to flatten it, using a specialist hammer. After a little while, she decides that it really isn't the right size after all, being too narrow, and returns it to the drawer of silver wire, saying she will find another use for it. She clips off a length of thicker wire and the hammering begins again. Ellie hands the hammer over to me, suggesting that I flatten both ends. One will be the free end of the spoon's handle; the other will be soldered to the bowl. I hammer, the ends start to flatten and the silver is pleasingly malleable. The main shaft of the handle also has to be flattened. I have a go at hammering it also. After a short while Ellie picks up the silver and shows me that because I have not been hammering perfectly straight, the handle is starting to curve a little towards one side. She is able to correct it with a few well-directed blows. I continue to hammer my flat ends. That done, Ellie bends one of the ends on the mandrel, checking it against the spoon's bowl, saying that if it does not fit precisely, the two pieces will not solder together successfully.

When the handle and the bowl seem to fit well, we move on to doing the soldering. Ellie says that the only thing to do is to balance the handle carefully on the up-turned bowl, after brushing on some flux. She places two pallions on the join between the two. I then apply the flame. As usual, I realise that I shall not be able to see when and if the solder has run and how well the joint has been made. Ellie encourages me to direct the flame up inside the bowl. When she tells me to stop, and I have quenched the piece, Ellie examines it and seems pleasantly surprised: the solder has run evenly and made a good, clean joint. 'Beginner's luck',

I say. None the less, I am tickled pink. 'My' spoon already looks pretty good. It certainly isn't a botched amateurish thing. Of course, that is because Ellie has directed the making of it and I have just done a bit of bashing and heating.

Finally, the completed spoon needs to be polished. I start working it over the fine-grained paper and then Ellie shows me how to use the foot-pedal-controlled polishing tool. This has quite a pleasing feel to it, but one has to judge two things simultaneously – the pressure on the pedal, and the pressure of the rotating brush on the metal. One certainly does not need the foot control to be depressed fully. Equally, if the rotating brush is not held to the surface with adequate force, then it does not get the polishing done. I do a bit of the polishing and Ellie finishes it off much more efficiently and effectively. We agree that we shall leave the inside of the bowl with a 'brushed' finish, while the outside surface and the handle will be polished. Ellie finishes off my amateurish polishing, briskly and efficiently. The results are immediately visible, and thoroughly satisfying. My spoon is now complete, looking rather elegant, simple and satisfying.

My silver spoon

While ceramics, glass and wood involve the transformation of base materials into something unique and beautiful, the making of jewellery and silversmithing involves the transformation of materials that are already precious. Even the copper has its value and its aesthetic appeal. The difference is visible in the waste materials: wood shavings are not treasured, and discarded clay can be recycled. Where the jeweller sits at her bench a piece of leather is slung to catch the finest of dust and shavings from precious metals. Like the other crafts, silversmithing connects the maker with ancient practices and long traditions of making.

The studio is a modern and domesticated counterpart to the goldsmiths' shops and foundries of past centuries: the heat derives from a gas cylinder and a modern torch. Nonetheless, the application of heat in transforming metal from a hard to a pliable material connects us to the very origins of metalwork, albeit on a miniature scale. And yet the metal remains hard. My failure to saw even a modest disc of silver reminds us that the novice – at least this novice – has limitations. It is abundantly clear that my capacity to grip the metal at the bench is poor. Despite observing Ellie, I can find no satisfactory way to grip the small sheet of silver while I try to saw it. Gripping with my left hand is uncomfortable and ineffective. I cannot place my fingers the way that Ellie does. And if I try to do so, the metal will not remain stable. As a consequence, the saw sticks, and moves the piece of metal even more. I try to use the saw in a regular, even, upright motion, but I fail. I am reminded that in a one-day encounter in the studio, I can appreciate my own physical limitations, or the qualities of materials, but I cannot learn how to overcome my shortcomings or develop the specific skills and strengths.

The finished ring and spoon – modest pieces though they are – are intensely satisfying. The spoon in particular evokes a sense of 'real' silversmithing. I am also reminded that I do not find working with my hands at all easy. Admittedly they are small and weak. But that is not the main reason: there are many makers and workers with small hands. I think it goes to a more deep-rooted aversion to such manual activity, derived from a lifetime of cerebral activity. When I said to Ellie at one point 'These hands are really made for typing', I was not doing anything other than covering my mild embarrassment. But perhaps it captured something more personal, more closely tied to my abiding sense of self. It remains unusual for me to have physical objects that are invested with even a small part of myself. Other than photographs, I have never really made anything, and although there is craft knowledge in creating satisfying photographs in the darkroom, using traditional wet chemistry, there is not the same sense of physical *making* involved. Just as in other studios, there is a gratifying sense of entering a domain of long tradition. The jeweller's bench has remained virtually unchanged for centuries.

The silver of the ring and the spoon is simultaneously resistant and malleable. As I was reminded when I made my wooden spoon, use of the tools does not come naturally. In my hands, they feel alien. They are not extensions of an embodied competence. The tools resist my handling, and therefore the materials resist my working on them. Even though the silver is, in principle, workable, it has no intrinsic quality in the absence of a competent worker. In Ellie's hands, the silver reveals a nature that in my hands it does not. 'My' silver remains inert; her silver is responsive. My spoon is the outcome of tension; her spoon is always under control. (They are of course, physically, the same spoon.) As with my other exercises, I am conscious of my own body's discomfort. As in the glassblowing shop and the ceramics studio, my shoulders hunch. As I hold the spoon to smooth its edges, I realise that I am holding it all over the place. My physical work has none of the close control of Ellie's. As I have already acknowledged, a task apparently as simple as sawing to a line pretty much defeats me. Where my intention, and Ellie's instructions, should guide my actions, the execution of even the most basic of tasks is imperfect in predictable ways – tense, away from my close control, and inexact.

6

Looking and Observing:
Life Drawing

All the activities included in this book demand discipline and commitment. In the service of thorough enculturation through apprenticeship, they require the investment of many hours of repetitive practice. Skills are acquired and improved through the diligent pursuit of exercises, repeated many times over. Such apprenticeship is the reverse of 'artistic' or 'creative' self-expression. Indeed, self-expression is entirely subordinate to the mastery of technique. In the world of the arts, perhaps nothing exemplifies this better than life drawing. Drawing the human figure has – together with some other elementary exercises – been the 'academic' basis of fine art training for many generations. For many practising artists, it is a discipline to which they return, like a singer working with a teacher throughout the career, or a ballet dancer taking a daily class. For many amateur or part-time artists, the life-drawing class is a leisure activity.

I had no aspirations towards becoming a skillful draftsman when I decided to take a short but intensive life-drawing class in London. I signed up with Rachel Clark, who has run classes for many years and has a studio in East London, in the converted Spratts pet-food factory beside the Limehouse Cut (a canal connecting docks). Over four consecutive days, between about 10 am and 5 pm each day, I shared her studio with a group of other learners. I was a complete novice, and as with nearly all my learning activities, I had no prior aptitude: I have never distinguished myself at drawing or painting. There was, undeniably, an aesthetic interest in life drawing: it can yield quite lovely drawings by talented artists. It is also unquestionably difficult. For the amateur, it presents particular demands. For me, there were also more methodological issues. Drawing anything, and life drawing in particular, calls for especially close and careful *observation*. So – like the equivalent exercise in photography (Chapter 7) – this was an exercise in the visual *per se*: not a visual ethnography but an embodied exercise in observing and recording in its own right. Drawing is a valuable exercise for any ethnographers or would-be field researchers (Causey 2017). Many ethnographers find themselves using whatever means are at hand to record their observations. They make 'notes' graphically as well as through discursive field notes. In many contexts, photography and video are possible, and they permit the fine-grained analysis of practical and aesthetic activities. Many of us, however, have found ourselves making rapid sketches to accompany our more conventional field notes. I certainly did so from time to time when I was observing the work of the Welsh National Opera Company. Photography of rehearsals and performances is not normally allowed (unless done on behalf of the company for publicity purposes). And yet, on occasion, I wanted to try to capture the distinctive posture of a director or a performer. A sketch, however 'sketchy', could help to evoke something distinctive about the delicate dialogue of speech and gesture that occupies the interpersonal space of the rehearsal studio or the theatre. Sometimes it would be little more than a couple of lines that tried to capture a sweep of the arms, or the bend of the body, that seemed to signify attentiveness. We struggle to find words that do justice to such embodied work. A drawing can help establish that vital parallel between the embodied competence of the social actor and the equally embodied work of capturing it. Life drawing requires us to pay close attention not just to the outlines, shapes and volumes before us but also to the spaces *between* those things. It is, therefore, an apt analogue of ethnographic observation. Like all my other exercises, what is at stake is not the 'artistic' quality of the drawings I produced but the effort I put into producing them and my reflection on that process.

In prospect and in practice, the life drawing can be daunting. In the first place, it is usually done in a group – in my case, a group of eight or nine learners. Secondly, unlike several of the crafts I have described, there is, as it were, no guiding hand. The tutor is not physically 'holding the other end' of the charcoal, pencil or brush. The onus is entirely on the learner to make appropriate marks on the paper. Moreover, the novice's drawings are, in principle, visible to everyone else in the studio (although, as I shall mention later, the etiquette of the studio can limit critical comment). Consequently, the life-drawing class can be a setting of multiple exposure. The naked model is, of course, exposed to the scrutiny of the group, but each individual learner's efforts expose her or his competence to scrutiny. As the tutor circulates among the easels and inspects each drawing, and as each student glimpses the work in progress of others, the studio becomes an arena of visual evaluation.

Irrespective of the gender, age or appearance of the model, the gaze in the studio is dispassionate. It parallels the experience of nude art photography (Chapter 7). In both settings, the gaze is primarily concerned with light, volume, shape and contour. In the life-drawing class in particular, the analytic focus is on the shapes and spaces *between* objects and elements as much as on the body parts themselves. This is, yet again, a useful concrete metaphor for the conduct of ethnography itself. Mapping the spaces becomes a vital skill in all drawing, not just of the human figure, and is of fundamental importance in observing any given social setting. I realise in retrospect that I embarked on the life-drawing exercise with one unexamined assumption on my part, which seems to be an equally unchallenged presupposition generally. That is: the life-drawing class is aimed at producing realistic representations of the model. Not everybody aims at the academic drawing associated with fine art schools, and there are many styles on show in the studio I share with my fellow students. But the general assumption seems to be that drawings or paintings will be within the framework of realism. Such an expectation creates distinctive expectations and pressures. Drawings or paintings can be evaluated in terms of their verisimilitude – their capacity to capture an accurate likeness of the model.

On the first day of the course, I arrived at the studio a bit early, but found that people were there already, setting up their easels and organising their materials. There were no general introductions. I gained the sense several of the participants were regulars and knew each other already. I felt particularly marginal. Rachel greeted me and showed me to my easel. She got me a drawing board, set it up on the easel and took me over to a table laid out with materials. She told me to take ten sheets of sugar paper, some charcoal and a rubber. I wrote down what supplies I had taken: I would be charged for what I had used at the end of our course. There were nine easels grouped in a semi-circle. Although the studio is large, airy and light, it becomes quite cramped with nine people working at easels (although I seem to recall pictures of life-drawing classes in art schools that seem even more densely populated). One has to turn sidewise to sidle between the easels to go to get paper, make a cup of coffee or go to the toilet. Throughout the day, and particularly at the beginning, I showed myself up as something of a klutz, a bit incompetent just with the basic equipment and layout of the studio. I kept kicking the splayed legs of my easel or that of my neighbour and was always in danger of knocking one of them over. Even manipulating the clips that I'd been given to attach my drawing paper to the board seemed repeatedly to defeat me. I ended up crumpling the paper or letting the paper slide off the board. Everybody else seemed to be able to manage quite happily, but I supposed that it was just part of being a complete novice, lacking even the basic physical skills, with little sense of where I was and what I was doing, and so unable to manage competently.

For the first day we had a male model, I estimated him to be in his fifties. Rachel said that we would start with a series of five minute poses,

the most important thing being to 'get something down'. It proved
remarkably hard for someone like me with no skills and no instruction.
You look at the body, you try to capture something of it, but for the
untrained eye and hand, it is very difficult to get the right shapes. Yes,
you know that the shoulders are at an angle, the hips probably at a
different angle and the knees consequently at yet another. Yet gauging
those angles and then transferring that 'knowing' into marks on paper is
far from straightforward. Even though I suspected that it was a 'wrong'
approach, I began by drawing an outline, starting from some arbitrary
point, such as a shoulder, and then trying to fill in some detail. I had no
sense of building up a drawing from basic shapes and volumes. The
results were predictably poor. There was little or nothing that was
credible about my first drawings. The bodies floated uncertainly, with no
sense of weight or volume. Legs dangled from the body rather than
supporting it, and joints were poorly articulated. The whole appearance
was, at best, flabby.

We then moved on to a series of one-minute poses, which of course call
for lightning-fast sketching; sometimes the poses changed quicker than I
could change the paper at my easel. I was, however, determined to make
bold marks, filling the large sheets of paper, rather than tiny things
tucked away in a corner. To begin with, I was struggling physically: the
top of my easel was too high, and I found myself reaching up uncomfortably. As the day wore on, although I adjusted the easel to a more
sensible height, standing with my arm raised in an unaccustomed position
became quite tiring and stressful in itself. It is a reminder that each new
activity calls for a new posture and a new physical configuration. The
technically proficient body is not the most 'naturally' comfortable: grip,
stance, head and rhythm can all need special education and alignment.
For the novice, there is a recurrent danger of relaxing into something that
is comfortable but 'wrong', while what is 'right' can feel strange. Indeed,
the phenomenological estrangement of learning some new skill or technique implies an embodied reorientation. In this case, a new 'gaze' must
be accompanied by new techniques of the body.

Rachel circulated, pausing at each easel, to offer a few words of
comment. When she got to me and one of my first drawings, she paused
and said it was 'bold'. (It was certainly large.) But it was perfectly clear
how poorly conceived and executed it was. My drawings from the short
poses all had the same basic problems. My bodies were all too upright,
too straight, lacking tension. The poses that the model had struck were
quite 'dramatic' – the torso twisted, the arms extended and the shoulders
thrust forward with one hand on a knee, for instance. Those poses are
just right in challenging the observer to cope with those physical tensions
and turns, the foreshortening of limbs and so on, but it was precisely

what I was not doing. I was failing to map the key features of the body, to check carefully where the verticals were falling – seeing where the knees fall in relation to a vertical from a shoulder, or a foot in relation to a line from the chin. Like many studio skills, it seems elementary in principle, but hard to put into practice with any degree of accuracy. One or two of the one-minute poses yielded results. I had no facility to complete a rapid sketch in any detail, but just capturing something of the volume of a crouching body, the turn of a head or the line of a back is satisfying. At the time, and in retrospect, I felt that just one or two of the most rapid sketches were the least disappointing. Under normal circumstances, I would not have kept all those hasty sketches, but I did so, as they constituted one element of my field materials. They were 'data'.

The final hour of the morning was filled by two half-hour poses. Rachel explained that just because we had more time, it did not mean that we should draw more slowly. On the contrary, we should still draw rapidly in order to capture the essentials, but additional time should be spent on finding what needed correcting, and then correcting it. I was still struggling, still was not achieving the required weight and volume in the body, and there were particular features that I was really failing to come to terms with. In my sketches, the model did not look as if he was grounded: the body and the limbs seemed to float aimlessly. It was a reflection of what I was and was not doing. Because I had no confidence in drawing hands and feet, I was leaving them until last. So instead of the feet bearing the model's weight when he was standing, the legs rather tailed off. To begin with, I realised I was *not* paying sufficient attention to the structure of feet, and was sketching a generic appendage, which looked more like a flipper than a foot. As the day went on, I made much more of an effort, trying to capture the shape of his feet and toes in a few clear lines. The model actually had rather well-defined feet, with a pronounced heel and arch, which made the observation easier.

My drawings needed critical review, however. During the morning, Rachel stopped by my easel and stood next to me. She looked past me, at the model, and on my drawing she drew some simple shapes – boxes with clear dimensions and volume. With a few deft lines, she was able to capture the key solid volumes of the model's body: the torso; a head that sat properly into the neck and shoulders; hips and thighs that were properly articulated. Her assurance was impressive, and highlighted my own inadequacy. It was exactly the sort of correction and guidance that was needed, however. On my own account, I also had a rethink. I had never seriously done any drawing with charcoal before, and I decided I was not helping myself technically. I had selected thin sticks of charcoal to work with. I realised that I was using it in a way that was not satisfying, nor was it helping me to generate pleasing drawings. I was being far too tentative in my drawings. Rather than creating clear lines and shapes, I was 'dabbing' with my stick of charcoal, resulting in vague and tentative outlines.

Over the course of the first afternoon, we devoted ourselves to a single pose. This presented its particular challenges as blemishes and failings could not be excused by the lack of time. As the afternoon progressed, I was reminded of one basic principle of drawing: that it is alright to rub something out and do it again. As Rachel said to me at one point: 'Matisse said that it doesn't take very long to do a drawing or a painting, but it takes much longer to correct it'. It is one thing to see that a drawing is 'wrong' in a general sense; it is quite another thing to see precisely how to correct it. That was obvious at one point in the morning. The model had adopted a pose with his head held low. I kept getting my drawing wrong because I was not committing to placing the head low enough. I was placing the head on a neck, but on proper inspection (prompted by Rachel), I realised that nothing of the model's neck was actually visible. The head in fact came really low down onto his chest, while my first attempt was completely impossible anatomically. I was having parallel difficulties with drawing knees. Like all joints, knees are very important in life drawing. My initial attempts were pretty poor. It took some demonstration for me from Rachel: the knee is quite a large structure, and has its own box-like form, and it certainly isn't an imprecise and shapeless bend in the leg. If anything, it works better to exaggerate its size and structure a little. In turn, that calls for closer and more purposeful observation. Knees and feet are not necessarily noticed in everyday life, and in the absence of a repertoire of visual references, they can get overlooked. Hands are also difficult although we do notice people's hands in everyday life, and they have their own complex anatomy. They are, nevertheless, tricky to capture, and easy to caricature with a thumb and four sausages. I started to concentrate on knees. As I have indicated, I had begun doing very sketchy feet as well. Following the same principles as the knees, I concentrated much more closely and purposefully on the model's feet, which were well defined. I had confessed my problem to Rachel, who came over with her sketchbook to help me. But by the time she did so, she acknowledged that I had started to sort the feet out for myself. Not only had I paid much closer attention, I had also begun to find a way to define the structure of feet – the heel, the ball of the foot, the curve of the instep – with a few charcoal lines. Likewise, closer observation of the model's hands – and my own – helped me to reconstruct more plausible structures.

As I review my work at the end of the afternoon, I resolve to change my approach the next day. If nothing else, my drawings will be bolder, with stronger lines. I shall also need to follow Rachel's precepts, focusing on establishing the elements of the model's body in terms of 'boxes': the torso, the abdomen, the elements of the limbs. I also need to work much more on the articulation of the body. Arms seem to pose a particular problem for me. They should be properly articulated at the shoulder, and again at the elbow and wrist. My drawings of arms, on the other hand, seem to droop like limp tubes, never achieving any strength or volume. At the same time, my drawn bodies were not convincing. Although I could occasionally get things more-or-less 'right', I was failing to establish the geometry of the image, observing the verticals, assessing the angles or mapping the body's relations. As a consequence, limbs got too long, or tapered off feebly, sticking out at impossible angles. The entire anatomy could become impossibly distorted.

By the end of the day, I was tired. I was tired from hours of intense concentration, and I was physically tired from standing at the easel, with my arm and shoulder aching and my back and neck stiff. This is a recurrent feature of novice days. Postures are unaccustomed, while the anxiety born of incompetence leads to physical tension. It is hard to 'loosen up' physically and personally. The short poses with which each day begins is one way to try to loosen the body and the drawing simultaneously, but tension can readily reassert itself.

The next three days followed the same pattern: fast, changing poses and then half-hour poses during the morning, and a single pose occupying the entire afternoon. I shall not continue by rehearsing all the details of the subsequent three days, although such a recapitulation might well capture one important feature of this and similar kinds of learning: repetition is one of the key motifs. I have noted that before but, appropriately enough, it merits repetition itself. We learn the kind of embodied techniques I am describing through the discipline of doing 'the same' exercises again and again. Such drilling can help to instil practical methods, and helps to translate them from matters of self-conscious effort to a more firmly embodied competence that can be relied on. Repetition and the discipline of drill does not mean, however, that things are repeated mindlessly. Repetition in the studio is akin to the process of rehearsal in the theatre or the opera studio. Each reiteration should be an occasion to learn, to try out and to put into practice what was learned last time. Like the conduct of ethnography itself, which can also be repetitious, it is a developmental, iterative process. At least – in both cases – that is the ideal. As I can attest, and so can many other learners, it is one thing to acknowledge and recognise one's errors but another thing to fix them. So in practice, repetition can involve making the same mistakes, or having the same blind spots. It is, I suspect, perfectly normal for 'progress' to be patchy rather than a smooth progress from failure to competence. Novices like me can quickly regress, losing their grip on techniques and methods, and reverting to their untutored style. For my brief excursion into life drawing, I certainly regressed as well as progressing a little.

By the second day, I felt less apprehensive going to and arriving at the studio. At least I knew that any humiliation would remain a private sensation. Although Rachel visited each easel in turn, and offered helpful, positive commentary, the overall atmosphere of the studio was thoroughly non-judgemental. This, of course, contrasts with the 'crits' of student work that is characteristic of the modern art school. Fine (2018) writes vividly of the ceremonial order of the 'critique' in postgraduate fine art (MFA) programmes in the United States. He describes it as being both 'routine and explosive' (p. 141). It is routine, in as much as it is a fundamental aspect of art education, and explosive, in that it can be akin to a degradation ceremony, with potentially wounding observations from teachers and other students. It is also a rite of passage to be survived. In Rachel's studio, there is no such overt, public critique. In these lessons, there is little overt comparison between the students or criticism of their work. Indeed, there seemed to be a degree of civil inattention in the studio, each participant preoccupied at her or his own easel. But as I moved from my place to get more paper, to go to the toilet or for refreshment breaks, I could hardly avoid glimpsing the work on other easels. Some of my fellow students were producing admirably strong, characterful drawings or paintings. But others seemed to be having problems similar to mine: they were producing images that – to put it unkindly – could have been produced from an artist's wooden lay figurine. Like me, they had failed to invest their bodies with any tension, weight or structure. In fact, one might have learned a little more from comparing learners' successes and failures. As I look around the studio, I can see much more accomplished work than mine, and some that seems to display some of the same weaknesses.

On the second day, our model was a young woman. So perhaps the experience was closer to a stereotypical view of life drawing, given how 'the nude' is often interpreted in the history of Western art. In practice, the experience of drawing a male or a female model is much the same. Self-evidently, the basic anatomy differs. But there is, at least on this occasion, one subtle difference. Our model is a young woman with a slender body. Doing justice to her appearance – even though it is not intended to be a portrait – suggests specific technical issues. The previous day's male model had a rounded belly, and it was relatively easy to draw his robust appearance. With the male model, emphasising the joints such as knees, and striving to convey a degree of bulk, was fairly straightforward. Trying to do justice to a more slender female body can be trickier.

Female model: 5-minute pose

I have, as I said, resolved to be more bold and resolute in my approach today. With thicker charcoal in my hand, I attempt to tackle the morning's short poses in a more purposeful way. I do not necessarily try to do complete sketches of her. I concentrate on getting on paper a few key elements. At the same time, I try to capture things with a smaller number of more decisive marks and lines. Some aspects of the female model can make that more satisfactory, and to some extent more aesthetically pleasing. Seen from behind, it is satisfying to capture the curves of the spine, the hips and the buttocks, for instance. So I concentrate on some 'simple' outlines, using the charcoal in clear, more decisive lines. Some of the rapid sketches feel like improvements, others much less so. Today, as on all four days, I kept even the most rough and inaccurate sketches as documentary evidence of my learning activities. I am not proud of them, and I fold them discreetly to hide the worst efforts from inspection by others. As with all my exercises in learning, I remind myself that it is the process and not the product that is important for me (although manifest successes would be nice).

The second afternoon involved a three-hour pose. Rachel encourages us to do two things during these longer sessions. First, to pay attention to the model's surroundings – the seat she is sitting on, the fabric and the background. The rapid sketches of the morning tend to be of bodies, or fragments of body, in space. The requirement to draw a more 'complete' representation creates its own further challenges. Second, Rachel enjoins us to complete the shading on the body. One cannot get away with just an outline drawing. Shading of course creates volume, and conveys a stronger sense of underlying anatomy. In principle, the representation of light and shade seems self-evident. In practice, it is yet another task of observation. Light and shade follow the subtle contours of the body and the characteristics of light as it falls on skin. There is often a halo of reflected light among the shadows as well. Like all aspects of our drawing, therefore, 'shading' demands close, sustained and careful observation. The danger, which I no doubt fell into in several ways, is to add shading in a generic manner – adding shade where one assumes it 'should' be, rather than paying properly close attention. Translating light falling on skin, hair, fabric and so on into monochrome tones, using charcoal (or graphite), requires an estimate of the relative tones. One has to try to establish the values: a certain amount of squinting ensues. I am moderately satisfied with my afternoon drawing of the young woman. It does, up to a point, do her justice, in that it does not make her look ugly, or her body ill-favoured. It is not perfectly convincing, and it has called for a good deal of erasing and correcting. But after two hours or so, it is done. As I did on day one, and as I do on the subsequent days, I spray the drawing, and all the other drawings of the day with fixative: I need to keep them for further reference and without that fixing the charcoal will smudge badly. At the end of day two, as I make my way home across East London, and as I dictate some field notes into a digital recorder at home, I am pretty exhausted.

My experience of regression returns on the morning of day three. I finished the second day feeling I had made progress. But I find myself looking at yet a third model – another man – and a large blank sheet of paper. I had thought that I had found a way of managing the short poses of the morning, but now I could find no way to make a mark. I stood there, more or less transfixed, clutching my stick of charcoal. I forced myself to make a start. It is the value of the morning's short poses that they require *action* and not reflection or contemplation. The model was doing some quite dramatic, even extreme, poses. Athletic though they were, I found it hard to capture some of his poses. I was certainly repeating previous errors: the body was too straight, with no tension in the limbs, the torso or the abdomen. Even when I was consciously checking the angles and the verticals, I was failing to put those principles into practice. Rachel came to stand by me, and by the side of my drawing, she quickly drew in a schematic representation of the 'boxes' that summarised the pose. I said to Rachel that I thought I had lost it completely that morning. Encouragingly she said, 'Well, you know, press on and you'll find a way and it will come back'. She reiterated her advice that it is better to err on the side of exaggeration, 'You know, don't be afraid of exaggerating; probably you're not, and it will be better than not [doing so]'.

As the morning progresses, I manage to get into some sort of rhythm. But I still struggle with some basic issues, and eavesdropping on other learners suggests I am not alone. I am still struggling with the overall proportions of the model's body. My particular problem is a tendency to make the legs too short and too slight. This reflects a failure to 'map' the model and my drawing accurately, despite the fact that I am diligently *trying* to establish the verticals, estimate the angles and assess the overall dimensions. Using my charcoal stick, I am trying to use the length of the model's head to measure the torso, the legs and arms, and to drop verticals from key points (such as joints). But despite Rachel's encouragement to 'exaggerate' if need be, my efforts remain cautious and my drawings sometimes (not always) fall away at the bottom of the sheet of paper. Even when I think that I have got the various angles and alignments more or less correct, Rachel can point out that the gap between one knee and the other is too wide, or that the angles of the legs are not quite right. The legs still do not look convincing, not really appearing to have any strength, or be capable of bearing any weight. It is all too easy to draw what one thinks rather that what one actually ought to observe. But I am developing a way of coping. I started on Day One using thin charcoal sticks and I realised that the tendency with that is to do fiddly drawing, dabbing at the thing, hoping to get it right eventually rather than really looking and translating what I could observe in simple, structural terms. I therefore tried to do two things. Practically speaking, I shifted to thick sticks of charcoal, in trying to avoid making tentative, finicky marks, and aesthetically I decided to try to make bolder, simpler sketches. It is easier said than done, but by the end of the day, I did say to Rachel I thought I'd discovered what I was semiconsciously working towards, certainly not achieving, which was implicitly asking myself: How would a modernist artist set about drawing this structure? And the answer – well the answer for me – is: She or he would describe it in broad outline with bold strokes, bold shapes and certainly wouldn't get hung up on fiddly detail. The latter is the kind of mistake that many of us novices make. We focus on detail and lose a sense of the overall structure.

Male model: half-hour pose

It is terribly easy to concentrate on getting just one part of the body 'right' rather than establishing the overall structure. I certainly have a tendency to start with the torso, getting those proportions, getting the chest and the rib cage, then getting the pelvis more or less sorted out and then embarking on the legs almost as a secondary thought; then embarking on the arms as a third thought. One has to start somewhere, but that is not a recipe for success in the long term, because that means that very often one has not mapped properly the relative positions say of elbows, wrists, knees, ankles, feet and so on. Beginning means *not* starting 'somewhere', but starting to establish an overall structure. It is not easy to translate intentions into actions and translate those actions into well-formed marks on paper, as opposed to making sense in one's mind. I realise that sometimes in attempting to create a bold line, I was actually over-exaggerating it and overdoing it – turning the drawing into something like a generalised abstract, rather than a naturalistic repre-sentation of the model in front of me.

On my last day, day four, I again regress, once more feeling that I have no idea of how to begin or how to go on. The male model, as normal, begins with five-minute poses. I respond with five minutes of dithering. Having previously decided to revert to thicker charcoal and bolder marks, for no obvious reason, I start more tentatively with thin sticks. That did not help me to overcome my hesitant start. Our model was the same man as on Day One. As the quick poses went on, I started to regain such modest confidence as I had gained previously. I again decided to concentrate on just a few aspects of the model, trying to capture some key shapes. I also made multiple rapid sketches on the same sheets of paper. Those palimpsests are rather comforting, whereas the blank sheet can be intimidating.

At mid-day, Rachel announces half-hour poses. Had I been trying half-hours earlier in the day, then they would almost certainly have been a waste of time, as I would have got nowhere. Now I have regained sufficient feel for what I am doing to be able to pull off some passable work and two tolerable drawings. One in particular seems to me to work quite well. The model adopts a pose, lying on one side and clasping his arms across his chest. This time, given that it is a half-hour exercise, I decide that the first thing to do is to spend some time actually looking closely rather than immediately picking up the charcoal stick. As I do so, I decide that the overall composition consists of three major triangles – one defined by the model's prominent hip, the second defined by the two arms together and the third by the top thigh. I also look carefully at the model's head, trying to judge just how low it is in relation to the torso. Having done so, I then try to estimate the relevant angles, holding up my charcoal stick. I try to establish the overall angle of the back and the shoulders (which I cannot in reality see). I then make the angle a bit more definite, in a way that feels exaggerated. Experience so far suggests that I have a tendency to reduce such angles, with the consequence that I straighten up bodies, and end up with bodies that float in no particular space, rather than occupying their own volume and having weight. Within the limits of my relative competence, it works. When I have been working on it for a while, Rachel stops by my easel in order to comment. She is complimentary, quietly saying 'beautiful'. But as I look at it afresh, I say to her 'But this arm is thoroughly unconvincing'. I seem to have a recurrent problem with arms. Legs have quite complex structures, and it is relatively easy to capture that to some extent: knees turn out to be large and complex; the muscles of the leg create lines and volumes of their own. But arms are often less overtly structured, while the shoulder can seem to lack clear structure too. If I am not careful, therefore, the upper and lower arms can look just like a pair of linked sausages. The obvious solution is, in the longer term, to pay more attention to the structure of the arm, and to pay attention to the elbow: although it is a much smaller structure than the knee, in just the same way it has a distinctive structure, better attention to it would almost certainly improve the drawing. On this occasion, I rub out the offending arm, and try to give it greater clarity and definition. My effort is a slight improvement this time, which is obviously a step forward, although it still seems a bit of a weakness. If I were to continue and take this further, it is obviously something I would work on. As it is, Rachel's quiet approval of this drawing is gratifying.

The other half-hour pose is a standing one. The problems and solutions here are the same as before: I realise that my verticals, horizontals and angles are still not precise enough. I am starting to appreciate the general principles more thoroughly (though at an elementary level). But putting them into practice remains demanding. I realise that if I can get the basic volumes and angles more or less right, then the drawing will carry a certain conviction, and if they are not right, then no amount of careful drawing of detail will ever rescue the piece. If therefore I can map the cardinal points, such as knees, shoulders and elbows, and establish the right angles between them, then the overall shape is a convincing one. That is not the whole story, I realise. It is also hard to get the body to stand or sit convincingly, with a drawing that gives an impression that the legs are supporting the body's weight, or a body that is apparently seated on a stool, not just floating above it. Rachel suggests to all of us that we ought to concentrate more on the pelvis, and getting the feet properly grounded. The model adopts a pose similar to one he gave us on Day One. I look as closely as I can. I try to concentrate on getting the pelvis and the legs sorted out properly. I fail completely. I try to see where it has gone wrong. I check the angles with my charcoal stick. I look again as carefully as I can. But the result on the paper, on the easel before me, remains disappointing. I scrap that effort completely. It seems beyond redemption. I start again, trying once more to get the lower part of the body right, and so building upwards rather than working downwards. As it happens my easel faces a mirror behind me. It is a salutary experience to look back and inspect a drawing in the mirror. The change of view highlights a great many things immediately. Whereas the proportions and volumes can look pretty convincing when facing the easel, the mirror image immediately throws everything into relief. Again, I can see immediately that there is a problem with the legs. They are too feeble and they are knock-kneed. I have produced the same problem with this pose that I identified in my abandoned attempt. I say as much to Rachel as she reaches my easel. As I would have predicted, she immediately checks my verticals and horizontals, and also checks the direction that my knees are facing. Somehow as she does so, the sources of the errors become more apparent. Getting the right space between the knees and the right orientation of the kneecaps makes an enormous difference. I was sure I had checked them and that I had got the relative positions of the feet and knees more or less right. But as soon as Rachel and I check them again, I can see that I was just plain wrong: not hugely wrong, but enough to ensure that the whole thing looks out of kilter. It is in one way profoundly frustrating, but looked at from a different point of view, if I don't learn to see my mistakes, I shall be bound to repeat them. If I can identify them, however annoying they may be, then at least I have some chance of rectifying them.

Days in the life-drawing studio were a powerful reminder of a recurrent theme throughout these exercises. That is, the 'bubble' of focused attention and collective commitment. The studio becomes a site in which – for a short but intense time – nothing else matters so pressingly. During the life-drawing days, therefore, one's concentration is focused solely on the task at hand. Even though the participants are not working together (as the cast of an opera or a play would), there is a strong, palpable sense of attention. While most of that attention is focused between each individual participant and the model, there is also an awareness of the fact that one's fellow students are also focused on the same object. In other words, the studio can be described in terms of a series of lines of force that run from each pair of eyes, each easel, centred on the model, while Rachel performs a mobile gaze that samples from those individual lines of scrutiny and their products. She moves, while the students and the model are fixed points, describing an arc of focused attention. The lines of the studio are circumscribed by the arrow slits between the easels through which each participant can observe the model. The tutor's mobility thus contrasts starkly with the students' immobility. And during each pose, and often between poses, the space of the studio is defined by those lines of attention that silently pierce the stillness.

Drawing is, or can be, a valuable exercise for the ethnographer. It is not necessary to enrol in a drawing class, or indeed to do anything out of the ordinary. But what any activity of drawing can promote is the willingness and capacity to *observe*. Drawing requires an active, embodied engagement with the physical act of observing. While photography and video are invaluable in many field settings, drawing is not just another mode of 'visual' data collection. It is a way of training the eye to pay attention to things, people, spaces and relations. Seeing and observing do not occur 'naturally'. Observation is acquired, and depends upon practical attention. Learning to 'see' competently and professionally requires a trained eye and socialised competence to translate what can be seen into something that is visualised and made into a phenomenon (Grasseni 2007; Gunn 2007; Roepstorff 2007). The ethnographic imagination deals in observation (sight) and analysis (insight) that frequently involves memory (hindsight) (Herzfeld 2007).

Causey (2017) encourages ethnographers to incorporate drawing into their fieldwork practice. He goes beyond the sort of amateurish stick figures or scribbled outlines that any and every fieldworker might try. His book is, therefore, partly a manual of instruction on *how* to draw effectively in the interests of ethnographic research. One does not need to reach Causey's level of competence in order to absorb the basic lesson: that we learn to 'see' what makes a drawing, and learning to observe is a significant discipline for the novice and practising field researcher alike. The hurried sketch, the captured gesture, in a field notebook can prompt memories and associations. Taussig (2011) celebrates the act of making rough sketches in one's field notes. He reminds us of how such images become part of the ethnographer's personal archive, and of their evocative power. He asks rhetorically why might the ethnographer use drawing rather than photography, and he responds:

> The most obvious retort to the question of why drawings in notebooks differ from photographs is that drawings – at least the ones I have in mind – fold organically into the writing in the notebook. You write on the page you are drawing on. It is all part of one process, while a photograph lies in another sphere altogether with a lot of technical junk between you and the world. I like the Luddite gesture of the drawing too, the almost purposely inept make-your-own in a world of packaged perfection saturated with Photoshop-enhanced pictures. (p. 21)

The palimpsest of written and graphic notes mirrors some of the kinds of 'observation' that the ethnographer cultivates, and the sources of memory that inhabit the ethnography. In the next chapter, I develop some aspects of the 'visual' as I explore the taking/making of photographs, and something of Taussig's 'technical junk' that mediates between vision and image.

7

Photography: Gaze and Resistance

Sometimes ethnographic exploration involves unlearning and re-learning rather than learning something new from scratch. The experienced singer who participates in a masterclass may be encouraged to set aside her habitual performance in order to re-think it; an experienced cook may have to relearn his techniques when coping with a new cuisine. In this chapter, I introduce one such learning experiment. It is all about photography. Now photography does not, at first glance, seem like the sort of esoteric activity I experienced through glass-blowing, wood-working or silversmithing. Everybody takes photographs, after all, and the pervasive use of smartphones means that photographs are being taken in greater numbers by more people than ever before. Since the invention of cheap film cameras by Kodak (the Brownie) in the 1880s and others, photography has been a mundane activity, with things like holiday snaps and pictures of celebrations being commonplace. At the same time 'art' photography has been increasingly recognised and valued. Prints by major photographers, such as Henri Cartier-Bresson, Anselm Adams, Alfred Stieglitz or Irving Penn are celebrated, exhibited and traded on the fine-art market. My aim here is not to emulate the most significant photographers of previous generations. But it is my intention to go beyond the truly everyday activity of taking 'ordinary' photographs, either with a camera or a smartphone.

This needs to be an exercise in re-learning. When I was young, I was a competent photographer. My father bought me a Rolleiflex twin-lens (TLR) camera, which takes twelve pictures per roll of 120 film. A TLR has two fixed lenses, one for viewing and the other for taking the picture. There is, therefore, no mirror movement, as in the single-lens reflex. The large negative size (6 cms square) gives images of high quality. The Rolleiflex was the workhorse camera for many professional photographers, used in the portrait studio or in the field. Many press photographers used them: they were robust and reliable cameras. A very good amateur photographer himself, my father also taught me how to develop film and to print enlargements. We darkened the home kitchen, with blackout curtains left over from World War II. The acrid tang of photographic chemicals takes me back there, more than fifty years later. My original Rolleiflex still works, and I am very fond of it and the other TLRs in my collection. Nowadays, however, I use digital cameras. I use them for everyday purposes and for fieldwork. I also use my phone, chosen because it incorporates Leica photographic technology. I already owned a camera, which was more than adequate although by no means top-of-the-range. Contemporary digital single-lens reflex cameras (DSLRs) I find too heavy and cumbersome: I have small hands. So I use an Olympus PEN compact system camera, with two zoom lenses. It generates pictures of good quality with excellent definition. I try to resist the amateur enthusiast's desire for ever more expensive and better-specified kit, preferring to concentrate more on the photographs themselves than on the equipment. I came to realise, however, that while I was moderately accomplished at analogue film photography and the wet chemistry of my darkroom, I was not using digital photography at the same level of expertise. Like a lot of people, I suspect, I was using fairly sophisticated cameras only in Automatic mode. I was taking photographs with my middle-range Olympus equipment as if it were just a point-and-shoot camera. There were plenty of functions that I was not using, and not thinking about. So while digital photography was, in principle, more sophisticated and offered more control over picture-making, I was making use of so few of its functions that in effect my own photography was less sophisticated than when I was using analogue, film-based techniques. Consequently, I was determined to add digital photography and the use of my camera to my list of short-term learning activities. Partly because of my early experiences of film-based photography, I always think in terms of black-and-white images. Even when I am viewing a potential image in the camera, I find myself thinking about it in terms of monochrome images. I realise that this is yet another aspect of image-making that I need to keep in mind as I embark on my relearning and rethinking exercise.

These preliminaries are by the way, but they are necessary background information to what follows. As a sequel to my work on life-drawing, I also wanted to incorporate 'art-nude' photography into my renewed engagement with the craft. Having cast around, I found a 'photography school' that was handy for where I could live in South London, run by Ion Paciu, a freelance professional photographer, whom I engaged for a series of four days on a one-to-one basis, to include a class with a model in a studio. I shall not recapitulate all that we worked on, as it would be repetitiously descriptive. As I have already intimated, my themes include two major strands that are intimately linked. I have to unlearn some of what I could take for granted in photography at the same time as re-learning how to take photographs. In the process, therefore, I find myself losing control. Losing and finding control is something that runs through all of these exercises. Here it comes to the fore most explicitly, perhaps. It is especially relevant when the 'material' I am working with is not just inert clay, wood or metal (intractable as they can prove), but is a human model. I shall elaborate on this and other aspects of the 'field' experience as the chapter unfolds. I shall also move on to consider the making of photography more broadly.

Ion and I begin our time together in the course of a day on the South Bank by the Thames on a cold but bright winter day. In the morning, we spend some time in the coffee shop at the Southbank Centre (home of the Royal Festival Hall). He examines my small, modest camera next to his Canon DSLR. I do not think he approves. We need to go through the principles of digital photography. I understand the basics of exposure – about the relationship between aperture and exposure time (which I still think of in terms of mechanical shutter-speeds). But digital technology means that I have to think differently about ISO. Now I know that when I used film, the 'speed' of the film (expressed as ASA, DIN, or ISO numbers) was fixed: that is, its sensitivity to light. Once the film was loaded, then one of the variables was fixed (although it was possible to 'push' the speed by under-exposing and over-developing the film). An ASA of 100 meant a relatively slow film, such as Ilford's FP4, suited to bright conditions; at ASA 400 a film (such as Ilford's HP5) was more suited to situations with less light or where a quicker shutter-speed was advantageous and so on up to ASA 3,200 for low-light photography. Likewise, the aperture of the camera's lens was set in discrete f-stops. The lower the number, the wider the lens aperture, and vice versa. A lens might be wide open at f2.8 and fully stopped down at f16 or f32. Hence I can normally estimate an exposure by assuming the ASA, bright conditions, and then a default value of f8 at 125th of a second. The required actual exposure for any given picture can then be varied up or down from such a basic starting-point. But a digital camera changes that profoundly. The ISO can be changed continuously, and therefore for any one shot there are three variables to consider. As I was also raised on fixed focal-length lenses, the two zoom lenses I have with my digital camera introduce a fourth degree of freedom, which in turn affects perspective and depth of field. Ion can navigate the controls on my camera with little or no difficulty, while I need to make constant reference to the instruction booklet. I have to peer at the camera settings, rather than checking them and changing them in the course of framing and taking a photograph.

Ion and I spend the afternoon taking photographs together on the South Bank by the Thames, near Waterloo Bridge. The sun is still bright, dipping to the West and shining straight along the Thames. It casts long, strong shadows. Ion looks up towards the London Eye, the landmark giant Ferris wheel that is nearby. He says he can see two pictures there right away. He asks me why. I mumble about the light, and the *contre-jour* (back-lit) effect of the sun behind the Eye. He is as interested in the geometric patterns created by the shadows on the ground as by the Eye itself. I take two photographs, one concentrating on the Eye, one with much more foreground. For the Eye photograph, I automatically turn the camera to take a vertical shot. As the afternoon wears on, and in retrospect, I suspect I do this unnecessarily often. It makes my use of the camera clumsy, and puts the controls in more awkward positions. I can, after all, crop images afterwards. There is no point in adding to the practical work of taking a picture if I am unnecessarily fiddling clumsily with the camera itself, and making it harder to concentrate on taking the picture and getting the timing right.

I take a couple of pictures of the London Eye and the foreground shafts of light and shadows, and so does Ion. Then he quickly spots a lone man standing in the middle-ground. He is smoking. He is rim-lit. Ion quickly takes a photograph: he captures the lighting on the man, and the smoke as he exhales. By the time I have fiddled about the man has moved and is no longer so perfectly lit. I am too slow. I am looking at the camera instead of looking through the camera at the subject, and so I have much less control over capturing the image at the right moment. Not for the last time Ion says 'Too slow', and he is right. It is temporarily annoying, but part of a wider lesson I am having to learn. People are walking near the shafts of light, and ought to make interesting photos, as their shadows are cast long towards us. I wait fairly patiently. Frustratingly, I notice that people walk in the shadows, perhaps avoiding being blinded by the low sun. I get fewer images than I hoped, and none is satisfying.

Ion and I turn our attention to the people and shadows below us. We are on a raised part of the South Bank complex, while the river and the riverside walkway are below us. It is a very popular spot for photography of all sorts, including shots taken in the course of tests of new cameras, published in magazines for enthusiasts. We both spot a woman walking along the footpath towards us. She is wearing a red coat, which stands out against the pavement and among the mostly drab winter clothes of the other passers-by. Ion says that he likes to spot such patches of colour in the otherwise monochrome world of London. I do too. There is a patch of sunlight through which the walkers come and go. I try to capture the red coat just as it enters the shard of light. I miss narrowly. 'Too late' Ion says again. But when I review the images later, I see that in fact I pressed the shutter a fraction of a second too early. Trying to anticipate the moment, I took the photograph as the red coat itself was illuminated, but the women's face and head were still in the deep shade of the bridge. I should have taken several in order to capture that moment. As I know in theory and in principle, street photography is quintessentially about timing. It is, as Ion says at one point, all about being patient and 'waiting for the right moment'. But when the right moment happens, taking the photograph is also a matter of being decisive. That decisiveness is embodied, even in the way one holds the camera and manages the body. Ion on several occasions tells me I ought to be standing and ready 'like a sniper'. He adopts a highly purposeful pose, one leg forward, the knee bent – indeed just like a military position. The camera does not leave his line of sight, either. I keep making the same basic, lame mistake. When I want to check the settings on the camera, or when I need to apply something like Exposure Compensation, then I look down at the back of the camera. The effect is of course that it is now pointing towards the pavement, and so the readings change anyway, thus vitiating the whole move. I need, urgently, to stop doing that. To make matters worse, I discover later that I have accidentally taken several pictures of the pavement itself. They can be deleted instantly, but the effect is one of personal embarrassment. I have never done that since I was a child, and tilted our old box camera, taking photos of my own feet. In the days of film, of course, such blunders could not be deleted. One had to wait for the film to be developed, and the offending picture would be there among the prints.

And so I need to learn and re-learn not just how to use the camera and its functions. I need to integrate the techniques into my embodied competence. The camera must become an extension of my intention. Posture, gaze, timing – these must all be learned afresh. And above all I have to engage in the inner conversation with the demon of resistance: Why am I doing this? I am a grown-up Professor Emeritus. This is not easy, and it is expensive. I do not have to put myself through the minor humiliations and frustrations of learning, and I certainly do not have to feel so cold. By the end of my day with Ion on the South Bank, I can barely feel my feet. But the demon is also like a daemon in Pullman's *His Dark Materials* trilogy. Daemons there are aspects of a person's identity, manifested in animal form. The person and their daemon are inseparable. The demon or imp of resistance is a necessary part of me, without which there would be no investment of energy or identity. In its absence there would be no inner dialogue – or at least the dialogue would be different, and might lapse into self-congratulation (see Whitaker and Atkinson 2019a, b for more on the imp of fieldwork).

Sun and shadow on the South Bank

After this first foray, Ion sets me some 'homework', so that I can practise using the camera, especially working on exposure. I am to select a number of scenes in Cardiff, with different kinds of lighting conditions, and take a series of shots, changing the parameters and using the exposure compensation function. I start to feel a bit more 'like a photographer', a little more in control of my technique, although it still seems to take a lot of thought, and is very far from second nature. I do at least recognise – not for the first time – the value of being challenged by a tutor. It is forcing me to *think* about what I am doing and to do it with some purpose. After all, the technical issues are important: as we have seen, without some technical fluency, I am not capitalising on photographic opportunities. But working with Ion is encouraging me to think visually again. I take pictures that pay attention to visual motifs, such as colour, pattern and repetition. The photographs are not startlingly good in themselves, and I remain conscious of just how much of an amateur I am still. But the photographs are, for the purposes of this book, secondary to the processes of learning and reflection that inform and are informed by their creation. Systematically changing the exposure values means that I start to acquire new forms of control over the camera and over my picture-taking. Indeed, picture-making starts to become a more realistic description of what I am doing. I recall the dictum concerning photography and the 'decisive moment'. I have missed some potentially decisive moments, or at least good opportunities, because I cannot use the camera with complete and unselfconscious control. My new relationship with the camera is placing me in the position of being a complete novice once more. It is a stark reminder that one needs full familiarity with tools and materials in order to achieve one's desired results.

I develop a greater sense of 'being a photographer' in the course of a second day with Ion on the South Bank. The plan had been to practise taking outdoor photographs with a model. But when we met, Ion told me that the model had phoned to say she was unwell, and it had been too late to find a replacement. We started in the Festival Hall, with coffee. Ion suggested that we went out together. I knew that I would be inhibited in Ion's company, so I made an alternative suggestion. On my way from the bus stop, I was reminded of the fact that at street level behind the Festival Hall, is an outdoor food market. I had assumed it was a farmers' market. In fact it is all street-food and drink. So I said to Ion that I had a better idea. He could stay and work (he always has stuff to do on phones and laptop) and I would pop down on my own and take some photographs in the food market. I felt that I would be able to explore things better on my own, although it had been years since I had set myself such a task. I have taken photographs in markets and similar sites on holiday, and I have a few black-and-white images I took in an antiques market in Venice that I am very fond of (using my old Rolleiflex SLR). But as I stepped out of the Festival Hall I felt more empowered than I would have had we been together. There is something about the risk-taking of making street photographs that can lead in one of two directions: one can either feel quite inhibited and retreat into taking generalised snaps of the scene, or one can make a rather different and more positive commitment to 'being a photographer'. Luckily, I felt impelled towards the latter. Ion's idea had been that I should stop strangers and ask them if I could photograph them. So I took my camera in my hand, feeling very positive. And I started taking photographs. As I shall note, I managed to take some 'portraits', but I found myself veering more towards 'candids', in a street-photography mode. The important thing is that I felt confident in doing so. I did not only take 'portrait' photographs of strangers, but also did some more 'candid' shots, including workers at the food stall and cus-tomers inspecting the food on offer. So I suppose that it was a brief excursion into 'street photography', which is actually the genre I most like.

I took a photograph of one couple. The woman looked annoyed, and I thought her expression made it a possible photograph. I certainly do not think that she wanted to have her photograph taken, but I stayed focused on the couple for a little while, and squeezed the shutter just as she looked rather aggressively straight at me. I moved on and lingered at several of the food outlets. I did not always explicitly ask permission to take photographs, but I made sure that I was very visibly planning or preparing to do so. (Generally speaking, in any 'field' setting, people are more concerned with getting on with their everyday work than worrying about being observed.) Only one worker reacted by 'posing', putting on a cheerful grin and giving me a thumbs-up gesture. Perhaps she thought I wanted the equivalent of a 'cheerful cockney' image. So I worked my way round the food market. It was pretty busy, people inspecting the food and eating at every stall. I was really taking candid shots of people, workers, and clients. I did not think I was getting anything very special, and I had not really found anyone I wanted to stop and photograph. I quite liked some of the small groups of people, who might arrange themselves in various interesting configurations: but I never quite got anything I really liked at the time (or subsequently). So having gone on like that for a while, I decided that I had to make more effort, and take some portraits. Luckily, I soon came across a middle-aged man with strong features. The low sun fell on him with a warm light. I just accosted him directly: 'Sir may I take your photograph?'. 'Sure', he said 'So long as you don't want my autograph'. I took the portrait shot, just the one. 'Well, you could have my autograph if you like', I said as I thanked him. Almost immediately afterwards there was another, younger man, who was also on his own (it appeared) and was happily eating: 'Sir', I said, 'The light is perfect on you', and took his portrait. 'Oh, I thought you were going to say it was because I am so handsome!' he said. I said something in return, to the effect of 'dream on', and moved on. I felt it was easier to approach people having broken the ice, and as I moved around with my camera, I felt less self-conscious. I asked a woman who was serving at one of the food stalls if I could take her photograph. 'Of course you can', she said, and got on with her work. I took three of her, from different directions. I liked the way her face (which had an expression of concentration) was framed by the written pricelists and other aspects of the stall. She continued with her work apparently quite unselfconsciously. I carried on taking photographs, with varying degrees of success. I rather liked a sort of double portrait of two young, hipsterish men. The sun fell on one of them in an interesting way, creating a dynamic angle. I feel I am starting to look, to observe, and to think in terms of pictorial values, such as how the sun falls on faces and places.

On review I ended up with a few passable photographs, and perhaps one really decent portrait, although it could have done with a wider aperture, throwing the background further out of focus. But the most important thing was it was an occasion when Ion had challenged me, and I had challenged myself, to do something photographic that was slightly uncomfortable (though not totally alien). Nowadays one has to be careful about photographing people and places, even in public: more careful I think than when I was young, and there was less overt concern about privacy and security. It provided a different occasion for inner conversation with the fieldwork Imp: 'You don't have to do this, you know', it whispered. 'Yes, I do. I've signed up on this with Ion, and I am not going to chicken out now. Besides, I've paid good money for this tuition…'. 'But do you really have to do something potentially embarrassing?' 'Don't be silly, it's just other people, enjoying themselves on a sunny day on the South Bank. What could really be the problem?' For once the Imp subsided, and for once I felt once more like 'a photographer'. I am not a good photographer yet (or perhaps again), but someone with a right to have a camera in his hand, not taking tourist views of the Thames. But there were some 'real' photographs: with at least some sense of light, exposure and framing, and some degree of control over the camera's functions. I am still not fluent, and I am certainly not perfectly secure with my digital camera. But I am getting there.

Cardiff: learning more about exposure

Art nude

The most demanding as well as most satisfying photographic session was the day spent on art-nude photography. Ion had booked a large room in a building near Waterloo station. He was setting up the studio (background and lights) when I arrived, and he told me that the model, who he had not worked with before, would be arriving at about 11a.m. In the meantime, Ion demonstrates and explains the lighting set-up – a master unit attached to the camera and two flash units operated by the slave. It was a basic arrangement that I understood in theory, but had never used. When I was young I had taken portraits using old-fashioned metal reflectors and hot photo-flood bulbs, as my father had done before me. We discuss taking high-key and low-key photographs. I am pretty familiar with those as ideas. Indeed, it was part of my own purpose today to gain some experience of making images of both kinds. I recall with Ion that when I was a student I managed to create a very effective high-key portrait of a young woman partly by design and partly by accident. Having taken a well-exposed image against a white background, I found some extremely hard, high-contrast, Agfa paper with a high gloss and an extremely white finish. So when printed on that paper, the image emphasised her dark hair, eyes and eyebrows, and lips all with minimal shading. I am hoping that we can achieve something good in low-key too. It lends itself to a more abstract approach to the body – the light spilling onto shoulders, breast or hips, the face lit from the side. I really want to come away from today's activity with some presentable photographs, just as I wanted to leave the various studios with decent pieces of glass, ceramics, silver, and so on.

The model arrives at about 11. Her name is Michelle, but of course I fail to catch it the first time and have to ask again. Ion says that the models don't necessarily use their real name. Of course I do not need or want to know her real name but if we are going to spend several hours working together, I just felt I had to be able to address her politely. (I called her 'darling' just as often, I now realise.) Naturally, I have no idea about the normal etiquette of the studio with a model, other than the everyday courtesy of civil inattention to her nakedness when I am not photographing her, or when she is undressing. She is dark with long straight hair, wearing spectacles. In her plain outdoor clothes she looks like a dancer. Her skin is pale. She is about 5'10" tall. She removes her clothes and her spectacles. In retrospect I realise that I forgot all about the spectacles, and wonder if I would have included them in some of the shots.

We begin by simply setting up the lights and Ion and I both take some basic photographs of Michelle simply standing in front of the background, so that we can check the camera settings. She is standing in a relaxed, informal way. In the few pictures I take of her, she looks "normal", in the sense that her hair hangs loose over one shoulder, and her body is not tense. The lighting creates no particular effect, and the resulting photographs have no special merit, other than showing Michelle in a fairly natural manner and in fairly natural colouring (as opposed to the high- and low-key modes). We begin the more serious photography with low-key work. The main light, from the side, throws light on her body in outline. And her face is just picked out, almost as a single line of light on her nose, lips, and chin. Because no light is actually falling on the background, it appears black in the photographs, even though in natural light it is perfectly white. The flash ensure such a short exposure that anything not illuminated is thrown into complete shadow.

One of the great advantages of the digital camera is that one can see the results immediately. As Leslie (2015) summarises them, Benjamin's strictures on photography relate specifically to the temporal rhythms of film-based analogue techniques:

> The undiscriminating eyes of memory and cameras absorb more than is consciously perceived and record it all for later examination. Memory develops belatedly into understanding, just as a photograph snatches an image from time and presents it to the world again only after a process of development. (p. 34)

Nowadays an image can be inspected and evaluated immediately after it has been taken. Looking at the instant playback of the digital image is a mixture of instant gratification and instant regret. Ideally, of course, it informs the next image. But one is not always sufficiently in control of everything to live up to that inspiration. Some of the images I take in low-key mode look quite pleasing when I look at them in the camera soon after. At least, they look more or less how I would have wished. The model's skin is pale, but in the rim-lit shots it looks perfectly dark. I take some 'abstract' shots. Abstract here means nothing very intellectual. In fact it really means concentrating on and focusing on isolated aspects of her body. It means paying close attention to how the light falls on the body's contours – inevitably in this case, shoulders, breasts, hips and buttocks.

So herein immediately lies a central issue. In doing this studio exercise I am implicitly recapitulating a century of male photography of the female nude. I cannot do it with any great degree of technical competence, but I am forced (or have volunteered myself) into a mode of practice that is at least questionable. You see, I must inevitably think not just about 'the lighting' but also how the light falls on her breast or on her nipple. The 'abstract' images that I take are also decontextualised aspects of her body – her buttocks, her breasts. So is this just yet another expression of the stereotypical male gaze? Many of the classic photographers had relationships with their model. Often they were or had been lovers. Here I am with a total stranger, her time paid for, looking at parts of her as dispassionately as I can. It is not a matter of feeling or suppressing an erotic impulse. I do not feel embarrassment for either of us at the level of ordinary interaction. But the normal dialogue and memorising of fieldwork have yet another dimension. There are recurrent issues in fieldwork surrounding the dispassionate observer, the voyeur, and the engaged participant. Here gender and the body render such issues more pressing. But then my interest is primarily intellectual. I am not trying to become a photographer, although I would always like to do such things better. If I want to learn and to experience, then I have to surrender to the situation. Otherwise there is no point. As I have always told my teachers, I intend and try to do all the activities wholeheartedly. Here I must do exactly the same. It is no good resisting the very thing I am trying to learn about. So there is a sort of 'bracketing' process while I focus on the concrete practices I am studying. Moreover, I have to resist the temptation of intellectual snobbery. But self-indulgence...?

As the day progresses, Ion changes the lighting so that most of the images are in high key. Michelle poses more overtly. When standing she is almost always on tiptoe. At one point I say to her that it really isn't necessary for her to be *en pointe*, but she says she actually feels better doing it. I agree with her that it certainly creates very different lines, because it puts her legs, back and torso in tension. The overall result is the same anatomical effect as that of high heels. They totally transform the curve of the back, the tilt of the pelvis, and hence the carriage of the bottom. (But is this the sort of observation I want to cultivate?) In preparation for high-key pictures, Ion asks Michelle to oil her skin. This seemed entirely matter-of-fact, although the first bottle of oil he produced from his bag was no good, as Michelle said she was allergic to it. Another oil was acceptable though. She said she had occasionally used olive oil. She moved to one side of the room to apply the oil. She stood by an open curtain at a window with her back to us and her dressing-gown loosened from her upper body, hanging loose behind her. As the cool natural light from the window spilled round her, I took a casual photograph of her on my phone. It looked like the sort of figure-painting a Nordic impressionist might have painted. Her pale skin and the natural light meant that in many ways it was one of the 'best' pictures of the day. Her back was relaxed, not tensed as it was in so many of her poses. And the natural light was much kinder than the strong studio lighting. Perhaps I may turn my mobile-phone snap into a drawing or even a painting. There is good reason for oiling the model's skin. Under the lights it enhances any natural sheen; Michelle's pale skin looked almost translucent, like white alabaster, and oil emphasised the effect of the lights. The sheen is artificially beautiful, perhaps, but then it is all a matter of artifice.

Michelle does a lot of standing poses. She often poses like a dancer, and she adopts somewhat theatrical postures. The issue of posing now highlights issues of control. To put it at its simplest, I am (semi)conscious of not being in control of what is going on. I am not surprised by this, as of course I have no relevant experience. But I feel that the afternoon goes by at a pace that is too fast for me. Not that I want to potter along unduly slowly. But in retrospect I should have called for a pause to reflect on what we were doing and what I was learning. As Michelle went on posing and as Ion and I kept shooting pictures, I was the one with little or no control over what I was doing. To some extent, I realise, I was just firing the shutter more or less whenever the model and Ion settle on a pose. So he and I were taking photographs at about the same time. This is not a criticism of Ion or indeed a criticism per se. It reflects the reality of the event. As a result, however, I now realise that I was not fully learning to look and to see. If I were thinking about the technicalities and the aesthetics again now, I would (I ought to) be paying much more attention to the lighting: how the model's arms were throwing shadows, how we might want to be moving the lights or changing a reflector to alter the overall illumination of the body and the background. And I ought to have been thinking much more about framing the shots. When I review my photographs I can see that some of the framing 'worked', in that I have those aspects of the model I wanted to concentrate on framed and composed as I would have liked. But sometimes, not least from being lazy and careless, I have blundered, so that there is too much or too little space round her, or that the picture is poorly balanced.

Sometimes, quite consciously, I just photographed Michelle as she was posing with little or no concern for the background – not making sure she was always framed only against the white background – more as a documentary reportage of the overall set-up, and as a record of how Michelle was using her body. This was particularly the case towards the end of our session together. Ion became interested in Michelle's suppleness and was directing her to lie on the floor and to turn her back and her pelvis, so that there was an extreme twist to her body. She also lay on the floor arching her back. I found it unpleasing aesthetically, being too tense and too 'posed', although I could also see that some photographers and some viewers would find it interesting, as it displayed the athletic power and suppleness of her body. I therefore contented myself with taking some pictures that illustrate her doing that, rather than framing a well-composed photograph of her in the pose. (They illustrate her activity of posing rather than being photographs of her in that pose, if that makes sense.)

Earlier in the day I had shown Michelle a few sketches I had made, some from my life-drawing class, and at least one from a classic Edward

Weston photograph. Weston was one of the most important photographers of the body, and several of his pictures have given rise to similar images since he made them in the 1930s. She said of the Weston sketch 'Oh yes, everyone wants that one', and I admitted that it was a classic pose. She also said it was nice to be shown proper sketches, as she was normally only given stick figures. Anyway, during the afternoon we did some poses that were based on her sitting on the floor, including variations on the Weston pose. That naturally meant that I had to sit or kneel on the floor. It provides the right height for shooting, but my joints are not suited to such physical efforts, and it became quite difficult. Getting to my feet was not always easy! My knees hurt slightly for a day afterwards. My right hip was painful. There was, therefore, an ironic contrast between the model, moving and putting herself into a variety of poses, moving like a dancer, and me uncomfortably and awkwardly grovelling on the floor. This is yet another example of the dynamics of control: control over the body, control over the setting, control over the equipment, control over the photographic image. Ion re-arranged the lights, so that he attached a very large, soft reflector more or less immediately above Michelle, so that when she was kneeling, sitting or lying on the floor, she was evenly lit.

When I review the photographs I took at the end of the day, I am pleasantly surprised by some of them. Low-key images, which in principle I have always admired, have worked well in some cases. Because Ion had positioned the lights appropriately, there are pleasing images in which the background and the model's body are in deep shadow, and the lighting falls on her shoulders, breasts and flank. The lighting is, perhaps, the most 'artistic' or 'abstract', and the furthest from anything that might hint at more 'glamorous' images. I also like some of the less strained poses when Michelle was sitting and kneeling. Again, the images seem less forced, although they are equally posed. Now it is important to reiterate here: the quality of the actual photographs is of secondary importance, though a matter of personal interest. Like all the other activities reported on in this book, this is a matter of learning, and of reflecting on the processes involved. More, this is not in itself an exercise in visual ethnography. While visual ethnography in its various forms is an increasingly important aspect of the methodological landscape, this is not intended to be one. My particular exercise in photography was not a means to some other end. This is, if anything, about photography itself. It is an ethnography of the visual, not visual ethnography. Like the other exercises I am reporting, it is also an enactment of recapitulation. My tutors and I re-trace the steps of brief apprenticeships. In the studio, we reprise elementary procedures and more-or-less standard apprentice pieces. My 'homework' photography and the tasks I undertook with Ion are themselves exercises in basic technique. Their outcomes were not a major series of outstanding photographs. But – as I suggested above – they were much more significant in helping me to 'be' a photographer and to act like one.

Equally, in exploring nude-art photography, I am self-consciously recapitulating decades of the male gaze of the naked female body. It is, I repeat, a thoroughly un-erotic experience, both in the taking of the photographs and in reviewing them afterwards. Of course, in regarding Michelle's body as a series of technical and formal challenges, not least in concentrating on the light on shoulders, breasts, and buttocks, I am in even greater danger of objectifying the female, reducing Michelle to just some quite nicely lit body parts. However, my intention was not to be a male voyeur, any more than my work on opera was an excuse to watch operas for nothing (in rehearsal). This is an exercise to parallel my excursion into life-drawing. Drawing and photographing the body are not 'the same', any more than painting or photographing a studio portrait would be. But they do present parallel challenges and opportunities. They are, moreover, simultaneously topics for ethnographic reflection and metaphors for ethnographic work more widely. Most importantly, perhaps, they help us to 'see' the difference between seeing, looking and observing.

Apprenticeship of the eye

Observation is active. It is intentional. We may see or look passively without reflection. But observation calls for concentration. It is an activity in itself. When we write and teach about 'participant observation', it is common to stress the element of participation: understandably so, as the comings and goings of participation – including access, ethics, and social relations in the field – are demanding prerequisites to any fruitful research, but observation needs conscious reflection and active engagement. As ethnographers, we need to cultivate the capacity to observe. Serious photography calls for observation. It is not based on random, unmotivated snapping of anything and everything. In precisely the same way, therefore, ethnographic engagements require active commitments to observation as action.

Ethnographies of the visual are as important as 'visual ethnography'. This exercise, which complements others in the series, again focuses our attention on the tool (the camera) and its affordances. It is a question of technique. Technique is not 'mere' techniques, as if that were a cheap and superficial relation to the means of making. As we saw with Marcel Mauss, technique is pervasive. It implies embodiment and practical activity, the relationship between the tool and the actor, and the cultural basis of conventional actions. Cultural commentary on photography – especially by the most celebrated of writers – can prove disappointing, often relying on rather bland generalisations instead of precise commentary on the act of photography itself. Moreover the texts are often about looking at photographs rather than the act(s) of photography itself. Sometimes it seems as if a distinguished author despises photography even while writing about it. Walter Benjamin's strictures against 'mechanical reproduction' are well known (Benjamin 2015), even though – as his contemporary editor points out – he 'cultivated a photographic style of writing. Benjamin thinks photographically; that is to say, he conjures up the workings of self and memory in photographic terms' (Leslie 2015, p. 32). At the same time, Benjamin was critical of forms of mechanical reproduction, which he regarded as 'assaults on humanity', providing 'legible images of the dysfunctional relationship of technology, nature and the social world by which humans increasingly become mere props – an experience not reserved solely for the working-class "appendage to the machine..."' (Leslie 2015, p. 8).

Despite the influence of her essays on the subject, Susan Sontag (1977) displays at best an ambivalent attitude towards the subject, at worst a rather lofty disdain: 'The same photographs, considered as individual objects, have the bitter and sweet gravity of important works of art, the proliferation of photographs is ultimately an affirmation of Kitsch' (p. 81). In reality, it seems to me, the great majority of photographs lie nowhere near those two poles – of art and Kitsch. But perhaps it is the very artisanal nature of much photography that can elicit such an attitude. John Berger (2013) provides a more valuable critical insight, based as it was on his very close observation of photographs and his grasp of observation more widely. In a phrase that could equally well apply to the work of ethnography, he suggests that: 'Photography is the process of rendering observation self-conscious' (p. 19). Such observation, like the ethnographer's enhanced observation and focused concentration, is in the present. There are many reasons for 'the ethnographic present' as a convention in ethnographic writing. But one of them relates to the equation of the ethnographic present and ethnographic presence. Ethnographic observation represents an incursion, an interruption of, the flow of everyday life. Likewise, the act of photography is predicted on a temporal interruption. As Berger has it, again:

> The time content of a photograph is invisible, for it derives from a play, not with form, but with time. One might argue that photography is as close to music as to painting. I have said that a photograph bears witness to a human choice being exercised. This

choice is not between photographing X and Y: but between photographing at X moment or at Y moment' (p. 19).

That sense of interrupted time is what Cartier-Bresson (1999) famously encapsulated as the essence of the act of photography: 'of all the means of expression, photography is the only one that fixes forever the precise and transitory instant' (p. 27). In that regard, we can trace yet further the parallels between the act of photography and ethnography. Both record in the vivid 'present': the moment(s) of a photographic record and the instances of an ethnographer's observations and notes. The photographs and the field notes constitute personal archives. The ethnographer may return to 'old' field notes in the same spirit that one might go back to photographs from the past. For the sociologist or anthropologist, such revisiting may be the basis for new analyses and publications. Opening and reading one's field notes once more, especially after a lengthy period of time, can also be nostalgic. Like old photographs, perhaps a little faded, they evoke memory and emotion – not merely information. They can recall to consciousness a lost youth, and – like lost love – a period of intellectual and personal exploration. Recognition might mingle with chagrin, at times lost and times regained.

My reflections here echo those of Thomas Eberle (2014), who – writing on the phenomenology of taking photographs – suggests:

A camera in my hand changes the mode of my perception: commonsensical everyday gazes are substituted by 'photographic gazes' that focus on visual phenomena and are guided by the intention of taking 'good' pictures. There is not 'a' or 'the' photographic gaze but there is a great variety of such gazes, focusing on different motives, themes, arrangements, perspectives, and so on. (p. 314)

It is not just about taking photographs. It is about 'being' a photographer, adopting a 'photographic gaze' and making that an occasion for bracketing one's normal vision. 'Seeing as usual' (which is the counterpart of thinking as usual) gives way to a self-conscious mode of observation and recording, even if the resulting images turn out to be nothing out of the ordinary.

The practical phenomenology of photography, as described by Eberle, contrasts with the treatment by Bourdieu (1990), which characteristically uses photography as a means to explore something else (class, family, hierarchies of value) rather than studying it as a phenomenon in its own right. Describing photography as a middle-brow art (*un art moyen*) becomes a vehicle for Bourdieu's recurrent sociological interest in the cultural codes of social distinction. His 'middle-brow' arts include Jazz,

which also has its distinctive cultural niches and enthusiasts or aficio-
nados. It is, therefore, instructive to compare Bourdieu on photography
with Becker on Jazz (Faulkner and Becker 2009). Likewise, Becker's own
contributions of photography speak to the practical experience of *being* a
photographer and sociologist (e.g. Becker 1974). My contrast of Becker
and Bourdieu is deliberate here (see Peneff 2018).

Given the centrality of observation to the conduct of ethnography,
versions of an 'apprenticeship of the eye' (Grasseni 2007, p. 25) are
valuable exercises in their own right, and as part of the ethnographer's
own enculturation. We need to cultivate ways of observing. My brief
exploration of photography and my more intensive engagement with life-
drawing both encourage me to think afresh about looking and seeing.
The experienced photographer is not just 'looking at' the world, but
through the camera she or he is actively observing. That implies a
cultivated grasp of light and shade, of perspective, of background and
foreground. That in turn implies technical decisions: perspective is
dependent on the focal length of the chosen lens, or the equivalent setting
of a zoom lens. The aperture chosen will determine the extent to which
the background is blurred or in focus. The chosen exposure will imply
decisions about lighting conditions. Similar considerations apply in the
life-drawing studio. Simply looking at the model will not yield any marks.
The gaze must be purposeful and disciplined. The body is realised in
terms of its formal properties and structures. The spaces between things
(such as knees) are just as important as those body parts themselves.
Active observation is also attentive to the figure and the ground, to
perspective and to the play of light. In the same way, the ethnographer's
looking or watching should be transformed into the kind of observation
that means the capacity to notice phenomena and bring them to
consciousness.

8

The Craft of Ethnography

I begin this final chapter with a brief summary of yet another exercise, a commercial 'taster' class to introduce novices to perfume blending. I do so in order to recapitulate some of my specific themes, and to emphasise the significance of incarnate, sensory work. Writing of taste and smell (inextricably linked in nature), Michel Serres (2016) takes as one starting point the memory of a bottle of Chateau Yquem (one of the great sweet white wines from the Gironde region), as savouring it in retrospect leads to a characteristic reflection on the nature of senses and sensations. He contrasts sensory perception with language use. Language, he argues, deadens or anaesthetises the sensory. If language derives from what Serres calls the 'first tongue', then the second tongue encompasses taste, or sensation more generally. But as investigators we must tackle the distance between the two – between language and the senses. The latter must certainly be explored, and even celebrated, but therein lies the recurrent paradox – that we have no resources but language (in whatever medium) through which to analyse those sensations:

> No doubt because smell and taste differentiate, whereas language, like sight and hearing, integrates. The first mouth stockpiles, the second expends: words pile up in dictionaries, food accumulates, frozen, in cold rooms, like bank accounts; smells and tastes are transitory, evanescent, ephemeral, differential. The map is refined like delicate silk, or a spider's web, with neither stock nor total, a fragment of time (Serres 2016, p. 157).

Irrespective of Serres's particular and distinctive reflections, it is the case that in addressing senses such as smell or taste one is inescapably dependent on the resources of language to try to capture the evanescent.

Attention devoted to the senses invites a radical empiricism, reflecting a turn towards 'pre-textual' ethnography (Rakowski and Patzer 2018). But we cannot, as ethnographers, or as everyday actors, dwell only in a fog of sensory impressions without conferring on them some order, some cultural framing, indeed without naming them. Of the senses, that of smell is at one and the same time the most evocative, the most ephemeral and the most elusive. It does feature in 'sensory' ethnography, but often incompletely or obliquely. Stoller's monograph on the senses in anthropology (Stoller 1989) is characteristically skewed. He has remarkably little to say about aroma, as opposed to sound. His treatment is rather less revolutionary a perspective than might have been expected, given his general significance in the discipline. His programmatic statements were agenda setting:

> I suggest that considering the senses of taste, smell, and hearing as much as privileged sight will not only make ethnography more vivid and accessible, but will render our accounts of others more faithful to the realities of the field – accounts that will then be *more*, rather than less, scientific. (Stoller 1989, p. 9, emphasis in original)

Stoller also suggests that while anthropologists had permitted their senses to penetrate the worlds of others, they had been much more reluctant to let their own senses be penetrated by the sensory worlds of others. Yet he has little to say about smell. That is despite the fact that among the Songhay, among whom Stoller conducted long-term fieldwork, perfume plays a significant cultural part. For instance, he recounts an episode in which perfume plays a central role. Visiting a woman informant, and as instructed by her, he takes a vial of perfume by way of a gift. He buys *Bint al Hadash*. He does not tell his readers how he chose it, where he bought it, what its ingredients were or what it smelled like. His informant chides him, saying he should have brought her *Bint el Sudan*. The 'wrong' perfume is put away and Stoller is sent off to get the right one. On his return they sit outside her hut and the fragrance of *Bint el Sudan* fills the air. Yet although this episode is used to exemplify the significance of the sensory, Stoller shows surprisingly little interest in the olfactory phenomenon itself. He does not tell us why a particular perfume was the preferred one. Yet there was another story to be explored there. *Bint el Sudan* (Girl, or Princess of Sudan) was the most popular perfume in Africa. It was commercially manufactured by a firm founded in Britain for the colonial market. So, there are many lines of inquiry that might have been inspired by that episode – not least what it smells of (jasmine, lilac and lily) – and its cultural associations (femininity, power, even a form of exchange currency). The point is not to be especially critical of Stoller, who has done much to promote interest in sensory ethnography, but to point out a recurrent motif in much of the literature. The significance of scent is often asserted, but not necessarily investigated as a phenomenon in its own right. As so often, the phenomenon is lost.

Rasmussen (1999) is another author to gloss over the phenomenon. Writing of the Tuareg she discusses perfumes and incense, used to facilitate communication between people and spirits. She tells us that aromas mark boundaries as well as challenging them. But Rasmussen does not examine aromas as phenomena, while making a familiar distinction between scents and language:

> Aroma signs do not have the same logically semantic structure as linguistic signs because smells are traces that, unlike words, only partially detach themselves from the world of objects to which they refer. (p. 69)

The passage from olfactory sensation to language is certainly phenomenologically tricky. But that does not mean that the sensory should be glossed over. On the contrary, it commends purposeful and self-conscious attention to the phenomenon itself. If we are not careful, sensations such as taste or smell just become vehicles or pretexts for the anthropologist or sociologist to discuss something else, accessed via sensations while the senses themselves remain unexamined. Diffuse discussions of experience, emotion or affect do little to disrupt this tendency (see, for instance, Culhane 2017). Admittedly, the description of 'smells in themselves' is all but impossible. As Henshaw (2014) notes '...most modern European languages have an insufficiently developed vocabulary for smells' (p. 16). People who are not specialists frequently highlight sources of smells rather than their intrinsic qualities when attempting to describe them; they also tend to stress the 'hedonic' (pleasurable) quality of smells (Hernshaw 2014; Ergen 1982), rather than attempting to characterise the scents themselves. My own very brief experience brings home that phenomenological difficulty.

When we try to embark on 'sensory ethnography', we have to do so wholeheartedly. The sensory and the sensuous need to be addressed through a thoroughly embodied engagement. Sensory ethnography is not captured through the collection of narratives about sensations, nor is it done justice by a reduction to purely visual representation. Too often sensory ethnography turns out to be a gloss for photography and video-recordings. And, as we have seen, visual ethnography is not synonymous with ethnographies of the visual. In the same way, sensory ethnography ought to pay explicit attention to the nature of sensory phenomena themselves. When we turn to olfactory phenomena, then we are immediately confronted by their sensory power, and simultaneously by our difficulty in naming and recognising aromas. We certainly respond to smells in a way that depends on the olfactory sense. But to go beyond that demands both a phenomenological bracketing and sustained, focused

attention. While we may not 'naturally' (in the natural attitude) find
words adequately to describe scents, and struggle to 'place' individual
smells in anything resembling a well-ordered semantic space, it is clearly
possible to train social actors to do so, at least to some extent. But as
Classen, Howes and Synnott (1994) point out, commercial perfume
branding and advertising have nothing to say about what perfumes
actually smell like or what they contain: 'Instead, advertisements speak in
terms of 'enchantment', 'sensuality' and 'mystery'. Sometimes more
attention is given to the bottle which contains the perfume than to the
scent itself' (p. 189). It is little wonder, then, that when we try to think
about scent – even 'perfumes' – we lack anything much beyond the purely
hedonistic by which to do so. Indeed, a great deal of anthropological
writing remains annoyingly vague about the senses. In her overview of
'sensing', for instance, Culhane (2017) focuses on 'experience' and
'affect', with little to say on the specificity of sensory phenomena in
themselves.

Teil (1998) does provide us with a telling account of olfactory training
and the disciplined attention to scent. Teil took a short course in olfac-
tion, associated with the appreciation of food, rather than focused on
perfumes. The participants in Teil's class were required to follow the
same smelling protocol in the attempt to reeducate the brain. We are prone
to respond to sensations of smell in terms of evocation: such impressions
need to be suspended and replaced with more precise, technical terms. One
needs, she explains, to be re-trained to deal only with the olfactory
information at the moment it is experienced. The participants, isolated
from one another, sampled a series of smells one by one. In doing so, they
needed to find ways to express those olfactory sensations, guided by the
instructor: 'In order to represent the olfactory sensation, and also to
communicate it, it is necessary to learn a language of description of the
sensation' (p. 510). This is a recurrent issue for any novice seeking to come
to terms with the domain of scent. Teil's instruction was based on a
classificatory system that furnished a new aesthetic that facilitated the
comparison of odours and the capacity to place new odours within that
classificatory scheme. The learning process was facilitated by the *malette à
odeurs* (literally, a case or cabinet), that laid out the smells in a structural
way. That arrangement is taken up by Latour (2004), basing his discussion
on Teil's fieldwork, who considers the classificatory arrangement to be an
extension of the actor: 'As far as progressive sensation is concerned, the kit
is coextensive with the body' (p. 207). Allowing for Latourian hyperbole, it
is the case that in all the studio settings I observed and participated in, raw
materials, tools and bodies comprise an ensemble, including the perfume
studio described below (see Jacob and Grabner 2010 for an overview of
studios as spaces of work). The discussion of a similar perfume-training

event by Muniesa and Trébuchet-Breitwiller (2010) also demonstrates the phenomenological demands on novice participants and authors alike in accounting for scents. Teil's initiation and my own learning exercise are a reminder that the phenomenological reduction, rendering phenomena strange and hence available for self-conscious scrutiny, is not an instantaneous event. It is not a *coup* analogous to a sudden *coup de foudre* or 'strangeness at first sight'. It is something we have to work at, if only to get beyond immediately superficial experiences and responses. Instead, the most thorough form of inquiry is *not* simply to identify 'strangeness' as something that a phenomenon is not (familiar, comfortable or agreeable), but to try to see it *for what it is*.

In the event, I took 'the same' class twice. The first visit happened at the suggestion of Mila Steele, who was at the time 'my' editor at SAGE. The second visit arose when a colleague, Dr Rhiannon Evans, said that she would like to try it too, in her case as a birthday treat. Both classes took place at the Experimental Perfume Club in East London, where there are regular classes and open studios where members can work on their perfume skills independently. My account is based on the first visit to the EPC. We arrived in good time, to find the studio arranged with a large square table, with seating for fourteen arranged round it. The back wall consisted of shelving, with row after row of small bottles of ingredients, and a blackboard that, looking like the 'specials' board in a restaurant, had some key words: names of some of the ingredients where the spelling was not obvious. At each seat was a blank preprinted workbook and a disclaimer form for us each to sign, most importantly relating to known allergies. Each work-place had a small digital scale, each with a small bottle sitting on it. The entire *mise-en-scène* spoke of a predictable order, of preparation and a carefully controlled environment. The young woman conducting the class identified herself as Emmanuelle, saying she was a professional perfumier who had worked for a major perfume house. She explained that during the first half of the course we would be introduced to twenty-five ingredients, and in the second half we would create our own fragrance that we would be able to take away with us. I was, and remained, conscious of the fact that my 'nose' is not as sensitive as many others', and although I can appreciate perfumes I am poor at picking up specific smells. Emmanuelle began by taking a sheaf of paper sampling strips and spraying perfumes on them. She did three, and asked us to label them A, B and C, and to write our impressions of each one in our workbook. Perfume A I could at least respond to, though in an impressionistic way. I wrote, 'it smells like my aunt'. I did not mean that literally, not least as I have no recollection of what my aunt smelled like, let alone what perfume she wore. I wanted to capture that sense of old-fashioned, powdery fragrance that one might have found on an older lady's dressing table. Emmanuelle revealed to us that it was in fact the most famous and classic fragrance of all – Chanel No. 5. Already it was a lesson in the extent to which one's cultural assumptions and associations do not necessarily correspond with blind sampling. I had difficulty placing B. I could certainly smell it physically, but it escaped my descriptive competence. It just seemed like a generic commercial perfume with no distinctive character. Some of the group members recognised it as one by Calvin Klein. The third seemed to be especially cloying and sweet. Again, several of the women in the group immediately recognised it as Angel by Thierry Mugler. It is one of the market leaders among women's perfumes. With the three commercial perfumes around the table, the studio was starting to smell a little like the cosmetics section of a department store. Each participant enacted sniffing, in that her or his attention to the task in hand was visibly enacted, wafting the testing strip, closing the eyes and looking round in the apparent search for appropriate analogies, descriptions or labels. The commercial session observed by Muniesa and Trébuchet-Breitwiller (2010) contained different styles of sniffing and responding:

> Some participants smelled the perfume quickly, then filled in their questionnaire in one minute (these worried the facilitator, as he suspected them of 'not smelling'). Many others smelled a first time for a few seconds, put the capsule down, then picked it up again once or twice during the questionnaire to smell again rapidly and finished within two minutes (these are the 'pros', the regulars; the facilitator considered them to be 'efficient'). Others kept the capsule in their hand, virtually under their nose, throughout the test, while filling in the questionnaire more laboriously. Finally, some started by smelling the perfume slowly, often with particular gestures, sometimes with their eyes closed, and started fairly late to fill in the questionnaire, repeating the process several times in a visible effort to concentrate. (p. 329)

After we had warmed up with the three commercial perfumes we moved on to the twenty-five ingredients. We were supposed to make notes in our workbook, writing down the name of each one and a brief description. What was noticeable was the extent to which Emmanuelle guided the group towards a collective description of each aroma, gathering up suggestions from round the table in a positive and encouraging way, and then synthesising them into what appeared to be the preferred description. The class therefore resembled many other kinds of pedagogic encounter, whereby the experienced teacher manages the discourse in such a way as to ensure a 'correct' outcome, as observed, for instance in school science lessons (Delamont, Beynon and Atkinson 1988) or in bedside instruction in clinical medicine (Atkinson 1981).

I do not go through all twenty-five ingredients here, but pick out several for comment. Number 2 was a case that illustrates the relationship between blind sniffing, recognition and naming. I could immediately notice – but not recognise – a very distinctive fragrance. It was familiar, but I struggled to place it. I wrote in my notebook that it was 'like lavender', though by no means a true lavender. Other participants also struggled to identify it, several visibly enacting 'searching' for the right answer. But it took Emmanuelle's prompt before any of us got there. She gave us the clue 'Earl Grey tea', at which point there was a small chorus of 'Of course!' and 'Bergamot!', the latter being the small citrus fruit used to perfume the tea leaves. So the ingredient came into focus, becoming – however temporarily – 'fixed' as a recognised 'something' rather than an un-named and vague sensation.

Number 4 prompted a variety of identifications that included 'grapefruit' and 'verbena', but none of the group came up with the right answer, which was 'blackcurrant'. Number 7 was immediately recognisable as 'fruit', and some specifically identified 'apple'. Mila suggested it smelt just like a Granny Smith, as indeed I agreed it did – once she had pointed it out. My own responses included the observation that I found it 'slightly acid'. I found Ingredient No. 11 particularly elusive. I wrote in my workbook that 'I don't get this one', though I added that it smelled of 'kerosene'. The 'right' answer turned out to the 'petals' and the ingredient itself to be Floral. Number 13 smelled to me to be an overpowering, cloying floral. It conjured up an image of lilies in a closed, airless room. I wrote down that it 'could be overpowering' and 'Miss Haversham'. Number 16 was something of a surprise. My notes said 'white flower' and 'domestic cleaner'. At first sampling I did not find it particularly pleasing. The other participants also seemed to have some difficulty in coming to a shared identification. Emmanuelle tells us it is Neroli, which is made from orange-blossom. It does not smell of orange, and I am puzzled, as I was under the impression I like neroli as an ingredient in perfumes. (This is an early intimation that ingredients can 'work' in combination with others in unpredictable ways.) Those were all 'top' note ingredients. Fragrances are conventionally described in terms of 'top', 'middle' and 'base' notes. The top are the scents that one first notices – floral, citrusy, or fruity – while the base notes are the heavy, lingering ones such as musk, leather or wood, while the middle give a fragrance depth or body.

The 'base' note ingredients are more readily identifiable as a general category, being darkly woody and leathery. They were not always easy to tell apart, though. My own exception was No. 25, identified for us as

Musk. Emmanuelle said that not everyone is physiologically able to smell it, and it seemed as if that applied to me. The sampling, describing and naming proceed at a fast pace. To get through all twenty-five, there is little time to discuss and reflect on each ingredient. Only two or three minutes were available for each. As in the other studios I report on, the course is carefully prepared and runs to a precise timetable. In order to shepherd all fourteen members of the group through the basic, introductory exercise, Emmanuelle needs to gather up the various volunteered answers and manage them so as to derive 'correct' answers that we can all appear to agree on, and so keep the class moving. Selecting and managing answers while maintaining pace and rhythm in the classroom is a recurrent feature of pedagogic encounters, and has been well documented in studies of classroom life. It is a tension in instructional encounters more widely: between spending time with each individual student and his or her needs and moving the class on as a cohort.

After a short break we moved on to the second exercise – blending our own perfume. Emmanuelle told us that of the twenty-five ingredients we had sampled, we should aim to use between eight and fourteen of them. That sounded daunting to me, although on reflection I realised I had no idea of what the 'right' number of ingredients would be. In front of us on the table were wooden frames containing small bottles of the ingredients, each rack shared between several participants. We each had a digital scale and a small bottle to hold our own blend. The small bottles hold ten grams. Apparently ingredients are measured out in grams rather than by volume. Emmanuelle explains how to reset the scale to zero after we add each ingredient rather than trying to do tricky mental arithmetic. I of course forget and have to recalculate each time I add one: an object lesson that doing things the right way, and following instructions, is the easiest way in the long run.

First we have to write the 'brief' for our own perfume. Some of the participants want to create something that evokes a particular time or place for them. I have no ideas along those lines. My own brief reads: 'Masculine, oriental, not too intense. A strong base and middle notes, and a top edge of bergamot. Can be worn by day or by night'. That was slightly tongue-in-cheek, but was also a fair representation of what I wanted to create. We were then instructed to list our chosen ingredients. We had to allocate a proportion of the overall composition to Top, Heart and Base notes. My ingredients were: Top (30%): bergamot, leaf green, blackcurrant; Heart (30%): five spices, neroli; Base (40%): amber wood, sandalwood, leather, musk. I realised even at the time that I was basing those choices more on the notes in the workbook (mostly owed to the suggestions of others) than from any realistic appreciation of what the various ingredients might smell like in combination. Emmanuelle came round the table to check each of our formulae. Looking at mine she said it was 'a good formula', but amended the balance to Top 20%, Heart 30% and Base 50%. I then had to translate those proportions into amounts for each ingredient, and then Emmanuelle recalculated the precise amounts out of a revised total of 9 grams, in order to leave room for any late additions. I made up my perfume, trying to concentrate sufficiently to keep track of which ingredient I had added. As it progressed, I was quite pleased with my creation, although I felt it was lacking in depth, a bit too light. I was reluctant to mess with it, as I quite liked it, but when Emmanuelle came round again to check on progress, I suggested that adding some more rose might give it a bit more weight. She agreed, and I added 0.3 grams. In the end, and following that small change, I was satisfied with my fragrance, blended from eleven ingredients. I named it *Don Paolo*, and bore my little bottle of *eau de toilette* home proudly. Later I ordered a larger bottle and have used it occasionally.

This brief exercise again reminds us of the possible significance of 'pre-textual' ethnography, in emphasising the work of the senses as incarnate ethnography. Here, it emphasises the creation of phenomena (in this case fragrances) through the actions of naming, so that 'recognising' becomes possible through individual or – as here – shared practices. Even 'obvious' fragrances (like bergamot) do not imprint themselves on our senses or on our powers of observation: they need associations and mnemonics. As described by Teil, and then by Latour, we also need some kind of semantic grid, in order to 'place' particular scents: the basic classification of 'top', 'middle' and 'base', and divisions such as 'floral', 'sweet', or 'woody' help us further to create phenomena that can at least be shared between actors. The 'creation' of one's own fragrance is not physically demanding – unlike throwing a pot or working with wood – and there is probably a strong element of chance as to whether the resulting fragrance is pleasing or not. (When I did the course again, my fragrance, intended to be more like a *fougère* and that I called GreenVelvet, was not very nice.) It does, however, demand intense concentration. Although the courses were pleasurable events, I could not just enjoy them, given that I was trying to do two kinds of things simultaneously – to describe or recognise the scents, and to describe the act of describing. And like the other exercises I have written about in this book, my work had two products: the fragrance and the texts. The texts consisted of my field notes and my written reflections, which I have not reproduced in detail here. As I shall reiterate in this concluding chapter, this is the essence of 'crafting' ethnography. That is, the homology between practical craftwork and the practice of ethnography itself.

Ethnographic work

Even fieldwork of this 'soft' sort is not easy. By soft here I mean fieldwork that is conducted in warm, dry, safe spaces: artists' or makers' studios, or theatres (as for my operatic ethnography). It does not compare with fieldwork in the streets, in isolated settings or in edgy environments. It does, however, have its own demands. Compressed field experiences, expressed in terms of hours and days rather than weeks or months, demand intense concentration. One cannot afford to let attention drift. A day in the studio calls for an almost equal number of hours of recollection, reflection and writing as we transform what we have seen, done or said into observations. That is, we make them available – at that time and for the future – for conscious and critical reflection.

Such practical work generates texts that are in turn the materials with which we work. They are not inert data, but intermediate or liminal products. They are materials to work with and to work on. Creating field notes and similar research materials is craftwork in itself. There are no protocols or procedures that can direct such work, and there are few available exemplars to follow. Like a lot of artisanal working, the ethnographer has to 'find a way' and to establish a method of working that makes production possible. We learn from some precedents, from mentors and from our own repetitious practice. To that extent, our notes are idiosyncratic, reflecting and incorporating distinctive styles of observation and reportage. More profoundly, we take those raw materials and their representations of mundane realities, and from them we shape something that is faithful to those realities, but differs from them. Just as the wood artist can transform a tree branch into a spoon; or as the glass-blower can take something as undistinguished as sand and transform it into a beautifully shaped vessel; or as the ceramicist changes clay into shaped, turned and glazed objects; the ethnographer does likewise. The craft rests in that transformative work. It depends on thorough acquaintance with those base materials, and trained experience in performing the creative, analytic work.

There is, therefore, a kind of *alchemy* in the pursuit of ethnographic understanding. It was, after all, the goal of the alchemist to find ways of transforming materials: most famously, turning base materials into gold. I do not mean by that it is a bogus exercise, or that it somehow contrasts with proper science. Indeed, alchemy and science were indistinguishable, and major figures in the history of science, such as Newton, practised alchemical experiments alongside work now regarded as pioneering science. As the contributors to the collection of essays edited by Dupre stress, there was no radical distinction between alchemy and artisanal craftwork in early modern Europe (Dupre 2014). The alchemists made significant contributions to the manufacture of dyes, porcelain and other materials. Rather, I stress the capacity of craftwork – and including ethnography – to transmute base materials into something special, or precious, that is significantly changed from these ordinary ingredients. In the case of at least one craft, the appeal to alchemy is also appropriate. In the history of ceramics, the discovery of how to make porcelain in Europe was one of the undoubted successes of alchemical research. And like glassblowing and silversmithing, it calls for transmutation through fire. Of course, the conduct of ethnographic research does not literally involve immolation in fire. But metaphorically speaking, one's initiation into fieldwork can be a baptism of fire, and field researchers are frequently transformed in the process. Buszek (2011) discusses how the everyday activities and products of 'craft' can become extraordinary through their incorporation into contemporary fine art; so too can the activities of everyday life become transmuted through ethnographic attention to their artistry, skill and performances.

Indeed, if we pursue the metaphor of alchemy, then the alchemy of ethnographic fieldwork simultaneously transmutes everyday life and transforms the ethnographer. We do not just craft our understandings and our analytic accounts; we also craft ourselves. The self-fashioning of the ethnographer involves the cultivation of a professional and personal identity *as* an ethnographer. Like the artisan or the traditional craftsman, the ethnographer finds an identity not just in what she does, but also in what she works on. Our selves are defined simultaneously by our methodological and theoretical orientations, *and* by our fieldwork sites. Anthropologists in particular become closely – often enduringly – associated with the culture and the people with which they have worked. So ethnographic fieldwork crafts our knowledge, crafts ourselves and helps us to craft the texts that inscribe those phenomena.

Crafting the self is not just a matter of intellectual transformation. As we have seen, ethnographic fieldwork is often an intensely embodied activity. We can be changed physically as well as being affected cognitively and emotionally. Each of the various disciplines I have described in the foregoing chapters implies a thoroughly physical, embodied orientation. Posture and gesture, focus and relaxation, breathing and choreography all demand more than a purely cognitive mode of learning. One cannot learn the required skills in the abstract first, and then subsequently put them into action. They are acquired through the physical learning that is simultaneously a matter of language and physical performance, acquired through imitation, trial-and-error and by following instructions. There is no mind/body distinction here, nor is there any in the conduct of ethnography. The participation of participant observation is an incarnate presence. Ethnographic work in studios also encourages us to focus on 'things', to take materiality seriously in fieldwork of all sorts:

> Rather than accepting that meanings are fundamentally separate from their material manifestations (signifier v. signified, word v. referent, etc.), the aim is to explore the consequences of an apparently counter-intuitive possibility: that *things might be treated as sui generis meanings*. (Henare, Holbraad and Wastell 2007, p. 3, emphasis in original)

Placing oneself in the position of being an incompetent novice is also a trope in describing ethnographers more generally. We are accustomed to using the trope of being a 'socially acceptable incompetent', as we place ourselves deliberately in the role of the outsider or the tyro, willing to learn but – at the outset – a cultural incompetent (Lofland, Snow, Anderson and Lofland 2005). This is sometimes misinterpreted to imply that ethnographers deliberately – and bone-headedly – avoid the acquisition of competence or expertise. Nothing could be further from the truth. Ethnographers become culturally competent as a consequence of their fieldwork, which implies a period of acculturation. But it is also a process of self-exposure. There is, or at least can be, a degree of cognitive dissonance involved. As graduate students, postdoctoral researchers, or as more senior academics, we can experience fieldwork in terms of a discrepancy between our academic expertise on the one hand and our novitiate status on the other. At a purely personal level, I was acutely aware of, and sensitive to, such personal divisions, which operated at an existential as well as intellectual level. Together with Emilie Whitaker I have published about this phenomenon (Whitaker and Atkinson 2019b). We expressed it in terms of 'the imp of fieldwork'. By the 'imp' we referred to that intrusive and persistent inner voice asking me 'Why are you doing this? You don't have to. You could be much more comfortable at your desk, just writing'. To be sure, the short-term nature of my illustrative incursions made deferred gratification perfectly tolerable. Fieldwork gives us stuff to write about, and therefore I knew I would feel even more comfortable sitting at my desk with something concrete to work with. Nonetheless, being a rank beginner in a studio, as a university professor in his late sixties, can sometimes feel uncomfortable and incongruous. I am used to at least the appearance of competence in my academic life. Being confronted by a blank sheet of blank paper and the need to draw a figure from life is a bit daunting, and the results far more than a bit embarrassing. Kneeling or half-lying on the floor, trying to take photographs as one's ageing joints hurt and lock up can easily conjure up that fieldwork imp. There is no dignity in it. There is little to be found in completely failing to saw a simple shape in a sheet of silver. Making a complete mess of trying to construct the most elementary of shapes on the potter's wheel is a matter of chagrin. Deliberately putting oneself in the position of complete novice and exposing one's incompetence is a form of self-exposure that, at the very least, encourages discomfort. Novices fall off (bicycles, surfboards), are clumsy and ill-coordinated (dancing, drumming), or physically inept (martial arts, cooking). But such ineptitude and its associated gaffes are integral to the overall process of learning. One's ethnographically induced exposure is equally a part of phenomenological estrangement and focused engagement with the phenomena.

Ingold's reflections on craftwork suggest that skilled, experienced practitioners do not construct their work according to a prefigured project: 'I want to think of making, instead [of a project], as a process of *growth*. This is to place the maker from the outset as a participant in amongst a world of active materials. These materials are what he [sic] has to work with, and in the process of making he "joins forces" with them, bringing them together or splitting them apart, synthesising and distilling, in anticipation of what might emerge' (Ingold 2013, p. 21, emphasis in original). Now Ingold's formulation here is too romantic, over-emphasising the maker's exploratory engagement with her/his materials. Many makers are engaged in the predictable, stable processes of repetition making. A potter creating a set of six matching coffee mugs or tea bowls is certainly envisaging each piece in terms of a plan or a project, probably in concrete terms based on a precedent or exemplar, in order to achieve predictable outcomes. Not all efforts will be perfect, and the potter or glass-artist might have to make more than the planned number to achieve a matching set or pair. But the degree of unpredictability should not be exaggerated.

There is a direct parallel once more with the conduct of ethnography. In preparing for and carrying out ethnographic fieldwork we do not normally have a fully fleshed-out research design. The spirit of open-minded exploration and discovery means that we do not conceive of the research project in terms of discrete hypotheses to be tested by bespoke experiments or their equivalent. Like the craftworker, the ethnographer engages with her or his materials (observations, talk, documents); she or he understands the affordances of those materials, working with the grain or against the grain of everyday life; relying on ingrained methods of investigation, s/he navigates the flow of the research environment; the craft of ethnography depends on our ability to *shape* our materials into written accounts or other types of representation (such as ethnographic films or hypertexts). Like the craftworker our understanding of and facility with materials and methods means that we have fairly good ideas about the sort of products we have in mind and the means to achieve them. We have well-established precedents to refer to and call upon, without copying slavishly.

Like the craftworker, we can 'lose ourselves' in the intense focus of fieldwork. Our concentration is on the current task(s) in hand: participating, observing, noting and recalling. We lose ourselves in the sense that we blot out any extraneous distractions. But we do not 'get lost', for that is quite a different thing. We lose ourselves in that positive sense that Solnit (2006) recommends, in being open to the unforeseen possibilities that our absorption implies. Our outcomes – like those of the craft worker – may be unpredictable but they are not without precedent. In a sense, each fieldwork endeavour is, like each new pot or blown vessel, a combination of circumstance and control. We know how to achieve our ends, and we know in general terms what that such outcomes will appear, while at the same time responsive to chance and the vagaries of our raw materials. That confluence of chance and control is also characteristic of ethnographic fieldwork and analysis.

There is one further aspect of ethnography's craftwork that calls for brief consideration. Craftworkers' production of artefacts creates a physical archive. They and collectors curate their body of work. They form a physical repository and a concrete memorialisation of the work. Ethnographers too create and curate their own archives. The studies reported throughout this book have, of course, led to my own archive of made objects. I have carefully kept the glass pieces that I made. Indeed, they are proudly displayed alongside objects of some major glass artists. The same is true of my little porcelain vessels that also share domestic space with studio pots by leading potters. My digital photographs are stored on disc, but some have also been printed as 12 by 10 inch enlargements (the old-school measurements I use deliberately here). From my life-drawing class I have a portfolio of all the sketches and drawings I made. Under other circumstances, many of the scrappy sketches and embarrassingly clumsy drawings would have been screwed up and thrown away. I have, however, kept them precisely because they are part of the record of my various attempts (many unsuccessful, a few less so). My wooden spoon is on display, as is my silver spoon, beside many more elegant artefacts by 'real' makers. The two perfumes I made are bottled as EDT sprays and share the shelf with more memorable fragrances by Penhaligons and Guerlain. There is, of course, a long tradition of ethnographers – anthropologists in particular – bringing back ethnographic memorabilia from their field settings. It is perhaps less common for such trophies to have been made by the ethnographer her/himself.

Such memorabilia are rarely the most important elements in the ethnographic archive. The most significant are surely the field notes, the notebooks and the transcripts of interviews. My own archive includes all the field notes I have ever made. My doctoral work in the Edinburgh medical school in the late 1960s was recorded in a series of reporter's notebooks. I followed the method I had learned as a student of anthropology at Cambridge: real-time notes and jottings on one page and the written-up version on the facing page in those spiral-bound notebooks. I have them still, and I used them for one exercise in re-reading field notes and thinking about them from a fresh perspective (Atkinson 1992). My field notes from my study of haematologists in Boston and in the United Kingdom are also carefully preserved from 1985. They are among the 'best' of my written-up notes. I was living alone in the city, and my working day always included several hours of writing up and my day's observations and conversations. The notes from Boston were written up in handsome cased notebooks bound in deep red and embossed with the arms of Boston University. I find them especially precious. I remember the effort that went into creating them. I wrote them up most carefully. They yielded a monograph I was proud of and that was well received (Atkinson 1995).

I will not go on to describe all my other field notes, except to acknowledge that my notes for the exercises reported in this book were different. I dictated 'processed notes', so there are no treasured notebooks. But as I have already confessed, my artefacts are my 'craft' archive for those activities. My point is this. When we think of our field notes and other memorabilia, they are more than just 'data'. They are never just inert items of information. We created them. From our observations and engagements, we crafted those texts. Already we were shaping our work: not only creating the intermediate texts of fieldwork, but starting to craft 'the ethnography' itself. When we work with them for the first time and when we re-read them later, we are not simply engaging with the texts. We conjure up the scenes and the actors that the notes refer to. Reading and 'analysing' (a misleading term in reality) those texts therefore involves an active engagement with them that is as much an act of personal memory. There is always far more in our memory than is contained in so many words in even the most detailed notes. Consequently, our archive of notes, conversations, interviews and artefacts are traces of ourselves. When we delve into that archive what we find is not just 'old data' but our former self/selves. The field notes made in the Edinburgh teaching hospitals evoke a young ethnographer fifty years ago. My Boston notebooks a thirty-eight year old, tenured and on sabbatical. My opera archive contains traces of an academic in his fifties who can afford to follow his curiosity. And so, in crafting our ethnographies we are also crafting and curating our selves (cf. Kondo 1990). That is, versions of ourselves that are specific to the context of the fieldwork and to the subsequent careers and representations of the project. For many of us, the trajectory of our ethnographies and of our ethnographic selves inscribes a kind of *Bildungsroman*: a story of personal development alongside our accounts of social exploration.

Less can be more

So, to return to the original themes of this book: I have attempted to demonstrate how we, as researchers, might seek to learn more from less, to collect fewer 'data' and to think more, and to do so more constructively. Furthermore, we do not need to seek out the exotic and the distant in order to explore. In undertaking ethnographic work it is easy to be seduced by the appeal of the far-away, or the deviant or the dramatic. While anthropologists no longer seek out the most remote of settings as a matter of course, they and many sociologists are attracted to field sites that are inherently 'other'. Studying deviance, or exotic activities is superficially attractive, and there is no doubt that much can be learned from social worlds that are self-evidently different and phenomenologically strange. Strangeness is certainly good. As we know, phenomenological strangeness is something to be cultivated, and ethnographic understanding is sought in the spaces between strangeness and familiarity. But cognitive and existential distance are to be achieved and cultivated. They are not 'givens', on the basis of surface similarities and distances, but are *achieved* through hard and painstaking work. So distance can be made nearby.

Likewise, ethnographic analysis is not guaranteed by the accumulation of mounds of 'data'. Novice researchers seem to spend far too much time collecting 'data', and almost as much time worrying if they have got 'enough'. That anxiety most often manifests itself in asking 'How many interviews do I need to do?' as if it were all just a matter of *volume*. Ethnographic excellence is never achieved by means of lots of data. It obviously matters not a jot if you have lots of field notes and/or interview transcripts if you have no idea what to do with them, or if you do not use them to think with. Consequently, crafting ethnography is not about collecting lots of under-analysed data. It is just as much about learning more from a little.

As an imaginative exercise I sometimes challenge myself, and graduate students, to select an encounter or an episode from the field notes (or more rarely from an interview) and to 'find' (in other words contrive) as much to think and write about as possible. That is not just a matter of attaching as many 'codes' as possible to a given excerpt, though I know that can help in some circumstances. Rather, it demands sustained thought. We have to keep asking ourselves: 'What is really going on here? How do they do that? How do the actors sustain it as an ongoing event? How is it ever different? What are the prerequisites for this encounter to be sustainable, culturally and interactionally?' These are not difficult questions to ask, with which to interrogate 'data', but that does not mean that addressing them adequately is in any way easy. It requires a very thorough knowledge of one's materials (data) and one's tools (ideas). The devil may be in the detail, but so too is ethnography's imagination. It is craftwork.

To identify ethnography with craft is not to downgrade the research. There is, after all, nothing bogus or inadequate about a well-made pot or glass vessel. The product of craftwork is robust and functional. The craft of ethnography is not a way to detract from its rigour or the value of the knowledge it produces. Craft of all kinds depends on technique, experience and skill. There is no contradiction between 'science' and 'craft'. As I outlined much earlier in this book, laboratory science depends on varieties of craft practice. The laboratory, like the studio, is an assemblage of apparatus, tools and raw materials. Science calls for practical, embodied activity and a significant element of tacit knowledge that is grounded in habitual recipes for action. At that level there is no inherent difference between science *as work* and craftwork. Craft, science and exploration (ethnography) are close relations in being based on parallel principles that include: experience, repetition, mastery of techniques, a close knowledge of the materials, the ability to observe closely, the ability to make something of what is to hand. The assemblage includes the array of resources and tools that are extensions of the worker's body, and that themselves embody her or his skills and everyday working practices (Harper 1987; Hamilton 2013; Keller and Dixon Keller 1996).

Crafting – ethnographic and practical – can also prove to be an exercise in deferred gratification. There are some activities that take shape in real time, or even instantaneously. It is, as we have seen, one of the distinct advantages that digital photographs can be reviewed immediately. Film photography was of the deferred kind. There was no image until the film had been developed and prints made from the negatives. But one must inevitably wait for the glass to cool, and for the pots to come out of the kiln. The glass can finally be handled, and will reveal its true colours. The pots can be handled and inspected; only then can one know if they have survived the firing process. Ethnography too can involve deferred gratifications. Like our craft pieces, it depends on the interactions of control, skill and chance. And during its sometimes protracted processes, we cannot be sure of its outcomes. There must be many moments when researchers in the field of ask silently 'What will I make of this?' Even the short, focused bursts of fieldwork I have based this book on involve a degree of faith. By virtue of its exploratory and unfolding nature, and in the absence of over-simplified 'findings', the final outcome – be it thesis or monograph – can be hard to foresee. The fieldwork and the preliminary stages of analytic reflection necessarily imply a degree of deferred gratification.

Equally, the identification of ethnography with craft practice is *not* an encouragement to abandon any or all of the more conventional canons of rigour. Craft is not a free-for-all. As we have seen, craft calls for careful, detailed work that is demanding of attention. Experience is based on apprenticeship that instils reliable technique. The craftworker's faith that she or he can 'do it again' is born of past repetitions. It may well involve experimentation with raw materials, techniques or forms. But such innovation is not a matter of aimless mucking about with no respect for precedents, methods and outcomes. Consequently, I personally have little time for authors who embrace innovation with insufficient regard for the past, who reject or ignore methodological conventions or who disrespect the craft. They are also in danger of disrespecting the graft – the hard work that goes into the making and the shaping.

We must also be cautious about appeals to ethnographic 'creativity' that place it in contrast to research methods as conventionally taught and practised. There is no contradiction between creativity and the craftwork of systematic, disciplined thought. Craftwork is creative. It is imaginative. Each craftworker develops her or his personal style. But he or she must also achieve competence in the techniques of the craft. Craft respects tradition, even when it innovates, and acknowledges the value of technique. It is by no means necessary to be hidebound by tradition in order to work creatively within and against it. I know that an endorsement of craftworking is easily seen as an elevation of Romantic modes of work and aesthetics (cf. Sennett 2008). Under the rubric of Arts and Crafts, or the early twentieth-century interest in traditional Japanese works – such as ceramics – it was easy to invest craftwork with special qualities. Hand-work contrasted with machine-manufacture, the former being endowed with a certain authenticity. The artefact and the maker alike, simultaneously, were contrasted with machine-based work and the factory model of industrial production. The individually made piece may have what Walter Benjamin described as the 'aura', as applied to an artwork in his case (Hanson 2008). The work and the worker alike can be endowed with special value. But it is important to avoid any over-romanticised view of craftwork or of ethnography. Adamson (2007) suggests that 'The romance of the work space, having been comprehensively dismantled (or at least critiqued) elsewhere in contemporary art, is still alive and well in the crafts' (p. 168).

It is true that each bears the distinctive traces of the creator. Be they potters or ethnographers, makers and writers shape their materials into characteristic forms. There is something of the maker or author in each artefact or ethnographic text. Equally, each work bears the imprint of traditions and genealogies into which the creator has been socialised. There is nothing mechanical or mechanistic in the making, and it reflects personal and local canons. But works inscribe their makers' identities and allegiances. Likewise, the ethnography is stamped with the interests and the style (intellectual and aesthetic) of the researcher/author. In concluding our ethnographic work we bring to the field the kinds of orientations and precedents that inspire and inhabit our work. But we do not follow them slavishly. Each and every study has its own characteristic style and flavour. We bring ourselves and our ideas *to* the field, and *from* the field we and those ideas are refocused. Our craft depends on repeated interactions between the field, our selves, our own ideas and the ideas of others. This is not aimless, it is developmental. Our creativity – the whole point of our research – is about setting off and finding a way. In many ways it is an act of faith, in which we are confident of *an* outcome, but may not know precisely *what* that outcome – or outcomes – will be. Hence my insistence on ethnography as craftwork and its products as craft artefacts. We know very well where we started, we know where we have reached, though we may not know precisely how we got there, or be able to retrace our steps. But, like the work of other crafts, productive thought and action do not spring from 'inspiration'; inspiration – insofar as that term can be used at all – derives from work. As ethnographies are made over time, so the successful ethnographer explores the properties of her or his materials, just as a worker in wood might examine the grain of a piece of timber, or the potter explore the properties of different clays and glazes. While the craftworker might (depending on the craft) speak in terms of seeing or finding a form that is already 'in' the material, and removing the wood or stone to 'reveal' the form that dwells inside, ethnographers cannot fall into the trap of thinking that their findings 'emerge' from the 'data'. The metaphor of finding form in the block or the material is just that, a metaphor. It will not work as a literal guide for those of us trying to make sense of a social world.

The crafting of ethnography depends on the craft(s) of writing. It is through our acts of writing, our textual practices, that we reconstruct social realities, actors, events and objects. If ethnography is a craft, then ethnographic writing calls for craft experience too. Indeed, the transformation of observation and participation into text is perhaps the most thorough craft-like activity we undertake. Just like any of our other craft-like activities, ethnographic writing calls for a thorough acquaintance with our materials, and with general principles of form and style.

Function and aesthetics converge in our understanding of genres, traditions and voice. Like the craftworker, we need to cultivate some sense of precedents and exemplars. In doing so, therefore, we need – as in all things – to act as *reflective practitioners*. I have written about these matters much more extensively elsewhere (Atkinson 2020) and so I will not recapitulate all of those arguments here. Rather, I shall offer some rather basic observations (see also Whitaker and Atkinson 2021). I want to establish a distinction between reflective practice and reflexivity. The latter term has been bandied about far too freely in networks of qualitative research and ethnography, with too many vague connotations. Many of those imply varieties of introspection, self-reflection and confession. Those orientations are also endowed with distinctive forms of personal research virtue. I am not interested in exploring this essentially narcissistic version of reflexivity or reflection. In my view, 'reflexivity' should be reserved for the universal and ineluctable fact that methods of measurement and means of representation help to constitute the phenomena that they define and describe. Ethnography is no different in principle from any other way of describing and representing social phenomena. We may well be committed to the view that it is an especially valid and ethical way of conducting research. We may think of ethnography as a way of life as much as it is a 'method'. It can be argued that participant observation is a research approach that is particularly faithful to the phenomena (see Atkinson 2015a). But for all that, we have to recognise that our research strategies and methods constitute the kinds of reconstructions that are possible. A symbolic interactionist stance yields a different perspective and analysis from, say, an interpretative anthropological perspective, or from a structuralist tradition and so on.

Reflexivity (in that sense of proactively reactive research) and reflective practice imply one another. A recognition that we constitute our phenomena through our methodological interactions with the social and material world enjoins critical reflection on what we are doing and how we are doing it. This applies particularly to our writing practices (and other modes of reconstruction/representation). How we choose to write is a major and fundamental aspect of our ethnographic craftwork. Now, the writing of ethnography gained special prominence in the 1980s, when 'the crisis of representation' was declared and debated (e.g. Clifford and Marcus 1986). Among anthropologists there was a widespread response to the effect that textual reflexivity and its implications threatened or even undermined the authority of the ethnographic monograph, for generations the bedrock of anthropological knowledge. While criticism of some of the assumptions inscribed in ethnographies was and remains valid, the announcement of 'crisis' seems in retrospect over-stated and misleading. Rather, I believe that a positive and constructive approach is called for. We now have a much more explicit and well-informed awareness of ethnographic writing in all its guises. Commentaries and critiques are now numerous. In the last analysis, the most significant issue is attention to our textual means to reconstruct and conscious control over what they can achieve.

Here I confine my comments to issues of analysis and writing that bear directly on craft – the ethnography of craft and the craft of ethnography. First, we need to pay close attention to everyday phenomena and action. Our overall texts must ultimately transcend descriptive accounts of our own and others' doings, but well-crafted ethnographic accounts should be faithful to the phenomena. Although his language is not my own, I commend Harry Wolcott's advice (Wolcott 2001). Wolcott in effect counsels against losing that sense of everyday life.

> For the most part, our inquiries are concerned with how other humans work through their everyday lives. Everyday experience is common to us all; our studies should not be pretentious. There is a fundamental fascination with the way other humans live, and our accounts should bubble with the stuff of life itself. When they do not – when accounts appear sterile and lifeless – how often is inattention to writing a fault? Our peculiar genius seems as often to take the life out of our studies as to celebrate the lives in them. (p. 111)

Now I do not fully endorse attempts to 'celebrate' lives, but I do appreciate the general spirit of Wolcott's remarks. Our writing must surely try to do justice to what people do, how they do it, with what resources. We need to find ways to do justice to the material realities of everyday life. That is not always easy. We have far too many 'ethnographies' that – strangely – pay insufficient attention to social activity, reporting only what people say in conversations or more formal interviews. But reporting on events, actions, things and sensations is not straightforward. Unlike stretches of transcribed talk, we cannot simply transcribe all of the multiple codings. (I realise that 'simply' glosses many technical issues and inherent problems.) If we are to attempt a phenomenological attention to the thingness of things, the materiality of materials or the surfaces of appearance, then we shall need to pay even closer attention to the descriptive power of the language we use. Likewise, in describing and analysing social action, skilled performance and embodied enculturation, then we also need to find ways of rendering them in written language. Self-evidently digital photography and video recording can go some way, and such images can be shared with readers and other analysts. But when it comes to synthesising and commenting on such phenomena, then I submit that the resources of ordinary language are required, indeed are vital.

Crafting ethnography, as I have argued, implies a thorough acquaintance with a wide range of phenomena and modalities of experience, encompassing the visual, the haptic, the olfactory. But more, they include some appreciation of *how* we grasp phenomena: through surfaces and textures, through heat and weight, through the play of light and shade, or through things' relative hardness or softness. Literally and metaphorically, these qualities are 'grasped'. As ethnographers we must grasp and reconstruct them as best we can, and sometimes as fully as we can. Seen from this perspective, a 'sensory' ethnography may encompass an almost decadent sensibility. It is characteristic of decadent literature of the *fin de siècle* that its authors, and through them their protagonists, are preoccupied (obsessed) with materials and sensations. Huysman's *A Rebours* (*Against Nature*, or *Against the Grain*, first published in 1884) is one of the classics of decadence. Its neurasthenic protagonist shuns the world, and in an enclosed environment is fixated on surfaces, sensations and things. It is a novella with minimal actions and maximum sensations. It is characteristic that one of the longest passages in that short book concerns perfume. Similar observations could be made about the works and personal life of Italy's decadent author Gabriele d'Annunzio. In fiction such as *Il Piacere* (*Pleasure*, first published in 1889) he explores sensuality, couched in a language that is itself a florid landmark of modern Italian. The author himself lived surrounded by excess of sensation – things, fabrics, perfumes – still visible in his residence at *La Vittoriale*, near Salò on Lake Garda. Now I do not suggest that we need to emulate decadent authors or their creations. We do not have to become neurasthenic or narcissistic libertines. But we would do well to pay some attention to their texts as well as their personal preoccupations, insofar as we need to write about, as well as reflecting on, the sensuous, the aesthetic and the sensory.

In addressing a phenomenologically informed ethnography, it seems important to strike some balance between 'external' and 'internal' reflection. That is, we need to provide adequate accounts of what is seen, heard, touched and otherwise apprehended. Equally, we need to grant sufficient reflection on *how* we grasped those phenomena, and how we learn to recognise, appreciate and describe them. Ultimately those are inseparable since phenomena are constituted through our active consciousness and our acts of construction. In terms of practical writing, it means striking a balance between observation and reflection, between the objective accounting for social realities and the more subjective accounting for the self of the observer-participant. That is why I am so wary of any attribution of 'autoethnography' to this book and its contents. In one sense autoethnography is a tautology. Every ethnography is totally dependent on the ethnographer herself or himself. Our interactions and observations rest inescapably on our socialised competences as social actors. We see, listen and hear; we touch and smell; we converse, reflect and memorise. The social world is filtered through our sensory, linguistic and cognitive grids. And so the self that is the 'auto' component is pervasive. We create the intertexts and the ethnographies. But my interests in this book are not primarily *about* myself. Hancock (2018) summarises the distinction rather well:

> Embodied ethnography differs from autoethnography in that the latter focuses exclusively on the researcher's personal experience in the field. Autoethnography focuses on the self, knowledge of the self, the dynamics of personal interest, and the investment of one's personal experience. Embodied ethnography, by contrast, is not about the meaning of personal participation. Rather, it uses full immersion into a particular world of study in order to fully understand the phenomena under investigation from the inside out, a vantage point that is inaccessible through observation alone.... (p. 156)

There is a world of difference between using our senses to document and understand a social world around us and a solipsistic focus on ourselves, not just as resources in the conduct of reflective research practice, but as the main (sometimes sole) topic – under the guise of 'reflexivity'. Crafting ethnography, like all craft, is therefore born of the repeated, exploratory interplay between the maker and her or his environment. That environment is simultaneously symbolic and material. It is a world of concrete, practical activities, artefacts and senses that are imbued with personal and socially shared significance. As ethnographers we overlook that duality at our own peril.

As I have argued elsewhere, it is important to 'rescue' ethnographic research from the mess of 'qualitative' research (Atkinson 2015b). The latter is highly popular, even fashionable, in many quarters, as is the more recent designation of 'qualitative enquiry'. The latter is closely associated with extreme versions of so-called reflexivity that substitutes self-gratification for sustained analysis. As I have tried to demonstrate in this book, and in the three previous books in the quartet, an ethnographic imagination should be based on a recurrent curiosity about the world around us. It takes a little reflection and a little more self-awareness to realise that the everyday doings of our fellow women and men are infinitely more interesting and more rewarding than we ourselves are. Ethnographers and other researchers are only interesting – if at all – because of their heightened understanding of the social and cultural world and what they achieve through that understanding. In the absence of sustained research-based knowledge, there is little or nothing to commend them as protagonists in their own self-narratives. While transparency of research is enhanced by researchers' personal reflections or 'confessions', we do not need to transform ethnographic writing into yet another genre of memoir or autofiction. The autobiographical must remain a way of showing how research is conducted in the real world, its contingencies and vicissitudes as well as its successes, but should not be an end in itself. Reflective practice might well include a degree of reticence and reserve.

References

Aalten, A. (2007) Listening to the dancer's body, in C. Shilling (ed.), *Embodying Sociology: Retrospect, Progress and Prospects*, Sociological Review Monograph. Oxford: Blackwell, pp. 109–125.

Adamson, G. (2007) *Thinking Through Craft*. Oxford: Berg.

Atkinson, P. (1981) The Clinical Experience: The Construction and Reconstruction of Medical Reality. Farnborough: Gower, 1981. 2nd edn, Ashgate, 1997.

Atkinson, P. (1992) *Understanding Ethnographic Texts*. Newbury Park, CA: SAGE.

Atkinson, P. (1995) *Medical Talk and Medical Work: The Liturgy of the Clinic*. London: SAGE.

Atkinson, P. (2006a) *Everyday Arias: An Operatic Ethnography*. Lanham, MD: AltaMira Press.

Atkinson, P. (2006b) Opera and the embodiment of performance, in D. Waskul and P. Vannini (eds), *Body/Embodiment: Symbolic Interaction and the Sociology of the Body*. Aldershot: Ashgate, pp. 95–107.

Atkinson, P. (2006c) Rescuing autoethnography, *Journal of Contemporary Ethnography*, 35, 4: 400–404.

Atkinson, P. (2013a) The mastersingers: Language and practice in an operatic masterclass, *Ethnography and Education*, 8 (3): 355–370.

Atkinson, P. (2013b) Ethnography and craft knowledge, *Qualitative Sociology Review*, 9 (2), 56–63.

Atkinson, P. (2015a) *For Ethnography*. London: SAGE.

Atkinson, P. (2015b) Rescuing interactionism from qualitative research, *Symbolic Interaction*, 38 (4): 467–474.

Atkinson, P. (2017) *Thinking Ethnographically*. London: SAGE.

Atkinson, P. (2020) *Writing Ethnographically*. London: SAGE.

Atkinson, P. and Silverman, D. (1997) Kundera's *Immortality*: The interview society and the invention of the self, *Qualitative Inquiry*, 3 (3): 304–325.

Atkinson, P. Delamont, S. and Housley, W. (2008) *Contours of Culture: Ethnography for Complexity*. Lanham, MD: AltaMira Press.

Atkinson, P., Delamont, S. and Watermeyer, R. (2012) Expertise, authority and embodied pedagogy in operatic materclasses, *British Journal of Sociology of Education*, 34 (4): 487–503.

Bachelard, G. (1964) *The Poetics of Space*. Boston, MA: Beacon.

Becker, H.S. (1974) Photography and sociology, *Studies in Visual Communication*, 1 (1): 3–26.

Becker, H.S., Geer, B., Hughes, E.C. and Strauss A.L. (1961) *Boys in White: Student Culture in Medical School*. Chicago: University of Chicago Press.

Benjamin, W. (2015) *On Photography* (Ed. and trans. E. Leslie). London: Reaktion.

Berger, J. (2013) *Understanding a Photograph* (Ed. and Introduction G. Dyer). London: Penguin.

Bosse, J. (2015) *Becoming Beautiful: Ballroom Dance in the American Heartland*. Urbana, IL: University of Illinois Press.

Bourdieu, P. (1977) *Outline of a Theory of Practice*. Cambridge: Cambridge University Press.

Bourdieu, P. (1990) *Photography: A Middle-Brow Art* (trans. S. Whiteside). Cambridge: Polity.

Brosziewski, A. and Maeder, C. (2010) Lernen in der Be-Sprechung des Körpers: Eine ethnosemantische Vignetter zur Kunst des Bodenschiessens, in A. Honer, M. Meuser and M. Pfadenhauer (eds) *Fragile Sozialität: Inszenierungen, Sinnwelten, Existenzbastler*. Wiesbaden: VS Verlag für Sozialwissenschaften, pp. 395–408.

Broth, M. and Keevallik, L. (2014) Getting ready to move as a couple: Accomplishing mobile formations in a dance class, *Space and Culture*, 17 (2): 107–121.

Buszek, M.E. (2011) Introduction: The ordinary made extra/ordinary, in M.E. Buszek (ed.) *Extra/Ordinary: Craft and Contemporary Art*. Durham, NC: Duke University Press, pp. 1–19.

Cartier-Bresson, H. (1999) *The Mind's Eye: Writings on Photography and Photographers*. New York: Aperture.

Causey, A. (2017) *Drawn to See: Drawing as an Ethnographic Method*. Toronto: University of Toronto Press.

Charlesworth, M. (1989) *Life Among the Scientists: An Anthropological Study of an Australian Scientific Community*. Melbourne: Oxford University Press.

Chernoff, J.M. (1979) *African Rhythm and African Sensibility: Aesthetics and Social Action in African Musical Idioms*. 2nd edn. Chicago: University of Chicago Press.

Classen, J. (ed.) (2005) *The Book of Touch*. Oxford: Berg.

Classen, C., Howes, D. and Synnott, A. (1994) *Aroma: The Cultural History of Smell*. London: Routledge.

Clifford, J. and Marcus, G.E (eds) (1986) *Writing Culture*. Berkeley, CA: University of California Press.

Collins, H. (1985) *Changing Order: Replication and Induction in Scientific Practice*. London: SAGE.

Collins, H. (2010) *Tacit and Explicit Knowledge*. Chicago: University of Chicago Press.

Crais, C. and Scully, P. (2010) *Sara Baartman and the Hottentot Venus: A Ghost Story and a Biography*. Princeton, NJ: Princeton University Press.

Crang, M. (2003) Qualitative methods: Touchy, feely look-see? *Progress in Human Geography*, 274: 494–504.

Culhane, D. (2017) Sensing, in D. Elliott and D. Culhane (eds) *A Different Kind of Ethnography*. Toronto: University of Toronto Press, pp. 45–67.

Dalsgård, A.L. (2018) Feet on the ground: The role of the body in pre-textual ethnography, in T. Rakowski and H. Patzer (eds) *Pre-Textual Ethnographies: Challenging the Phenomenological Level of Anthropological Knowledge-Making*. Canon Pyon: Sean Kingston Publishing, pp. 25–39.

Davis, K. (2015) *Dancing Tango: Passionate Encounters in a Globalizing World*. New York: New York University Press.

de Waal, E. (2010) *The Hare with Amber Eyes*. London: Chatto and Windus.

de Waal, E. (2011) *The Pot Book*. London: Phaidon.

de Waal, E. (2015) *The White Road*. London: Chatto and Windus.

Delamont, S. and Atkinson, P. (2021) *Ethnographic Engagements: Encounters with the Familiar and the Strange*. London: Routledge.

Delamont, S., Beynon, J. and Atkinson, P. (1988) In the beginning was the Bunsen: The foundations of secondary school science, *International Journal of Qualitative Studies in Education*, 1 (4): 315–328.

Delamont, S., Atkinson, P. and Parry, O. (2000) *The Doctoral Experience: Success and Failure in Graduate School*. London: Falmer-Routledge.

Delamont, S., Stephens, N. and Campos, C. (2017) *Embodying Brazil: An Ethnography of Disasporic Capoeira*. New York: Routledge.

Douny, L. (2013) Wild silk textiles of the Dogon of Mali: The production, material efficacy, and cultural significance of sheen, *Textile*, 11 (1): 58–77.

Downey, G. (2005) *Learning Capoeira: Lessons in Cunning from an Afro-Brazilian Art*. Oxford: Oxford University Press.

Downey, G., Dalidowicz, M. and Mason, P.H. (2015) Apprenticeship as method: Embodied learning in ethnographic practice, *Qualitative Research*, 15, (2): 183–200.

Dudley, K.M. (2014) *Guitar Makers: The Endurance of Artisanal Values in North America*. Chicago: University of Chicago Press.

Dupre, S (ed.) (2014) *Laboratories of Art: Alchemy and Art Technology from Antiquity to the 18th Century*. Cham, Switzerland: Springer International.

Eberle, T. (2014) The art of making photos: Some phenomenological reflections, in M. Barber and J. Dreher (eds) *The Interrelation of Phenomenology, Social Sciences, and the Arts*, Basel: Springer, pp. 311–320.

Ergen, T. (1982) *The Perception of Odors*. London: Academic Press.

Evans, J., Davies, B. and Rich, E. (2009) The body made flesh: Embodied learning and the corporeal device, *British Journal of Sociology of Education*, 30 (4): 391–406.

Faulkner, R.R. and Becker, H.S. (2009) *Do You Know? The Jazz Repertoire in Action*. Chicago: University of Chicago Press.

Featherstone, K. and Atkinson, P. (2011) *Creating Conditions: The Making and Remaking of a Genetic Condition*. London: Routledge.

Fine, G.A. (2018) *Talking Art: The Culture of Practice and the Practice of Culture in MFA Education*. Chicago: University of Chicago Press.

García, R.S. and Spencer, D.C. (eds) (2013) *Fighting Scholars: Habitus and Ethnographies of Martial Arts and Combat Sports*.London: Anthem

Garfinkel, H. (2002) *Ethnomethodology's Program: Working Out Durkheim's Aphorism*. Lanham, MD: Rowman and Littlefield.

Garfinkel, H. and Wieder, L. (1992) Two incommensurable, asymmetrically alternate technologies of social analysis, in G.Watson and R.M. Seiler (eds) *Text in Context: Studies in Ethnomethodology*, Newbury Park, CA: SAGE, pp. 175–206.

Gere, C. (2009) *Knossos and the Prophets of Modernism*. Chicago: University of Chicago Press (cap.).

Gladwin, T. (1970) *East is a Big Bird: Navigation and Logic on Pulawat Atoll*. Cambridge, MA: Harvard University Press.

Goody, E. N. (ed.) (1982) *From Craft to Industry: The Ethnography of Proto-Industrial Cloth Production*. Cambridge: Cambridge University Press.

Goody, E.N. (1989) Learning, apprenticeship and the division of labour, in C.W. Coy (ed.) *Apprenticeship: From Theory to Method and Back Again.* Albany, NY: State University of New York Press, pp. 233–256.

Grasseni, C. (2007) Skilled visions: Between apprenticeship and standards, in C. Grasseni (ed.) *Skilled Visions: Between Apprenticeship and Standards.* Oxford: Berghahn, pp. 1–19

Gunn, W. (2007) Learning within the workplaces of artists, anthropologists and architects: Making stories from drawings and writings, in Grasseni, C. (ed.) *Skilled Visions: Between Apprenticeship and Standards.* Oxford: Berghahn, pp. 106–124.

Haase, B. (1998) Learning to be an apprentice, in J. Singleton (ed.) *Learning in Likely Places: Varieties of Apprenticeship in Japan.* Cambridge: Cambridge University Press, pp. 107–121.

Hamilton, L. (2013) The magic of mundane objects: Culture, identity and power in a country vets' practice, *Sociological Review,* 61 (2): 265–284.

Hammersley, M. (2017) Interview data: A qualified defence against the radical critique. *Qualitative Research,* 17 (2): 173–186.

Hancock, B.H. (2018) Embodiment: A dispositional approach to racial and cultural analysis, in C. Jerolmack and S. Khan (eds) *Approaches to Ethnography: Analysis and Representation in Participant Observation.* New York: Oxford, pp. 155–183.

Hanson, M.B. (2008) Benjamin's aura, *Critical Inquiry,* 34 (2): 336–375.

Harper, D. (1987) *Working Knowledge: Skill and Community in a Small Shop.* Berkeley, CA: University of California Press.

Hastrup, K. (2018) Muscular consciousness: Knowledge-making in an Arctic environment, in T. Rakowski and H. Patzer (eds) *Pre-Textual Ethnographies: Challenging the Phenomenological Level of Anthropological Knowledge-Making.* Canon Pyon, Herefordshire: Sean Kingston Publishing.

Henare, A. Holbraad, M. and Wastell, S. (2007) Introduction in *Thinking Through Things.* London: Routledge, pp. 1–31.

Henshaw, V. (2014) *Urban Smellscapes: Understanding and Designing City Smell Environments.* New York: Routledge.

Herzfeld, M. (2007) Envisioning skills: Insight, handsight, and second sight, in Grasseni, C. (ed.) *Skilled Visions: Between Apprenticeship and Standards.* Oxford: Berghahn, pp. 207–218.

Hooper, M. (ed.) (2019) *The Story of Tools.* London: Hole & Corner.

Ingold, T. (2011) *Being Alive: Essays on Movement, Knowledge and Description.* London: Taylor and Francis.

Ingold, T. (2013) *Making: Anthropology, Archaeology, Art and Architecture.* London: Routledge.

Jackson, A. (2011) Men who make: The 'flow' of the amateur designer/maker, in M.E. Buszek (ed.) *Extra/Ordinary: Craft and Contemporary Art.* Durham, NC: Duke University Press, pp. 260–276.

Jackson, M. (1989) *Paths Toward a Clearing: Radical Empiricism and Ethnographic Inquiry.* Bloomington, IND: Indiana University Press.

Jacob, M.J. and Grabner, M. (eds) (2010) *The Studio Reader: On the Space of Artists.* Chicago: University of Chicago Press.

Jones, G.M. (2011) *Trade of the Tricks: Inside the Magician's Craft.* Berkeley, CA: University of California Press.

Jordan, B.G. and Weston, V. (eds) (2003) *Copying the Master and Stealing his Secrets*. Honolulu: University of Hawai'i Press.

Keller, C.M. and Dixon Keller, J. (1996) *Cognition and Tool Use: The Blacksmith at Work*. Cambridge: Cambridge University Press.

Knoblauch, H. (2005) Focused ethnography, *Forum Qualitative Sozialforschung/Forum Qualitative Social Research*, 6 (3), Art 44. http://nbn-resolving.de/urn.de:0114-fqs0503440

Kondo, D. (1990) *Crafting Selves: Power, Gender and Discourses of Identity in a Japanese Workplace*. Chicago: University of Chicago Press.

Lande, B. (2007) Breathing like a soldier: Culture incarnate, in C. Shilling (ed.) *Embodying Sociology: Retrospect, Progress and Prospects, Sociological Review Monograph*. Oxford: Blackwell, pp. 95–108.

Langlands, A. (2017) *Craeft: How Traditional Crafts Are About More Than Just Making*. London: Faber and Faber.

Latimer, J., Featherstone, K., Atkinson, P., Clarke,A., Pilz, D. and Shaw, A. (2006) Rebirthing the clinic: The interaction of clinical judgment and genetic technology in the production of medical science, *Science, Technology and Human Values*, 31 (5): 599–630.

Latour, B. (2004) How to talk about the body? The normative dimension of science studies, *Body and Society*, 10 (2-3): 205–229.

Lave, J. (2011) *Apprenticeship in Critical Ethnographic Practice*. Chicago: University of Chicago Press.

Lave, J. and Wenger, E. (1991) *Situated Learning: Legitimate Peripheral Participation*. Cambridge: Cambridge University Press.

Layton, P. (1996) *Glass Art*. London: A&C Black.

Layton, P. (2006) *Peter Layton and Friends*. Wellington, Somerset: Halsgrove.

Layton, P. (2012) *Past and Present: Peter Layton and London Glassblowing*. London: Halstar.

Lenk, S. (2018) The epoché, mindfulness and the body: Dynamics of a phenomenological experience in the field, in T. Rakowski and H. Patzer (eds) *Pre-Textual Ethnographies: Challenging the Phenomenological Level of Anthropological Knowledge-Making*. Canon Pyon, Herefordshire: Sean Kingston Publishing, pp. 171–195.

Leslie, E. (2015) *Introduction to Walter Benjamin on Photography* (ed. and trans. E. Leslie). London: Reaktion.

Lewis, J., Featherstone, K. and Atkinson, P. (2013) Representation and practical accomplishment in the laboratory: When is an animal model good-enough? *Sociology*, 47 (4): 776–792.

Livingston, E. (1986) *The Ethnomethodological Foundations of Mathematics*. London: Routledge.

Livingston, E. (2008) *Ethnographies of Reason*. Farnham, Hampshire: Ashgate.

Lofland, J., Snow, D.A., Anderson, L. and Lofland, L. (2005) *Analyzing Social Settings: A Guide to Qualitative Observation and Analysis*, 4th edn. Belmont, CA: Wadsworth.

Malinowski, B. (1935) *Coral Gardens and their Magic*. London: Routledge and Kegan Paul.

Marchand, T.H.J. (2001a) *Minaret Building and Apprenticeship in Yemen*. London: Routledge.

Marchand, T.H.J. (2008) Muscles, morals and mind: Craft apprenticeship and the formation of person, *British Journal of Educational Studies*, 56 (3): 245–271.

Marchand, T.H.J. (2010) Making knowledge: Explorations of the indissoluble relation between minds, bodies, and environment, *Journal of the Royal Anthropological Institute*, 16 (Special issue 'Making Knowledge'): S1–S21.

Martin, T. (2021) *Craft Learning as Perceptual Transformation: Getting 'the Feel' in the Wooden Boat Workshop*. London: Palgrave.

Mauss, M. (2006/1935) *Techniques, Technology and Civilisation* (trans. D. Lussier and J. Redding, ed. N. Schlanger). Oxford: Berghahn.

Meskus, M. (2018) *Craft in Biomedical Research: The iPS Cell Technology and the Future of Stem Cell Science*. New York: Palgrave Macmillian.

Muniesa, F. and Trébuchet-Breitwiller, A-S. (2010) Becoming a measuring instrument: An ethnography of perfume consumer testing, *Journal of Cultural Economy*, 3 (3): 321–337.

Nishizaka, A. (2020) Apperance and action: The sequential organization of instructions in Japanese calligraphy lessons, *Research on Language and Social Interaction*, 53 (3): 295–323.

O'Connor, E. (2005) Embodied knowledge: The experience and the struggle towards proficiency in glassblowing, *Ethnography*, 6 (2): 183–204.

O'Connor, E. (2006) Glassblowing tools: Extending the body towards practical knowledge and informing a social world, *Qualitative Sociology*, 29: 177–193.

O'Connor, E. (2007a) Embodied knowledge in glassblowing: the experience of meaning and the struggle towards proficiency, in Chris Shilling (ed.) *Embodying Sociology: Retrospect, Progress and Prospects* (Sociological Review Monograph). Oxford: Blackwell, pp. 126–141.

O'Connor, E. (2007b) The centripetal force of expression: Drawing embodied histories into glassblowing, *Qualitative Sociology Review*, 3 (3): 113–134.

O'Connor, E. (2007c) Hot glass: the calorific imagination of practice in glassblowing, in Craig Calhoun and Richard Sennett (eds) *Practicing Culture*. London: Routledge, pp. 57–81.

Paterson, M. (2009) Haptic geographies: Ethnography, haptic knowledges and sensuous dispositions, *Progress in Human Geography*, 33 (6): 766–788.

Paxson, H. (2013) *The Life of Cheese: Crafting Food and Value in America*. Berkeley, CA: University of California Press.

Peneff, J. (2018) *Howard S. Becker: Sociology and Music in the Chicago School*. London: Routledge.

Pink, S. and Morgan, J. (2013) Short-term ethnography: Intense routes to knowing, *Symbolic Interaction*, 36 (3): 351–361.

Pollner, M. (2012) Reflections on Garfinkel and ethnomethodology's program, *The American Sociologist*, 43 (1): 36–54.

Pollner, M. and Emerson, R.M. (2007) Ethnomethodology and ethnography, in P. Atkinson, A. Coffey, S. Delamont, J. Lofland and L. Lofland (eds) *Handbook of Ethnography*. London: SAGE, pp. 118–135.

Polanyi, K. (1958) *Personal Knowledge: Towards a Post-Critical Philosophy*. Chicago, IL: University of Chicago Press.

Qureshi, S. (2004) Displaying Sara Baartman, the 'Hottentot Venus', *History of Science*, 42 (2): 233–257.

Rakowski, T. and Patzer, H. (eds) (2018) *Pre-Textual Ethnographies: Challenging the Phenomenological Level of Anthropological Knowledge-Making*. Canon Pyon, Herefordshire: Sean Kingston Publishing.

Rasmussen, S. (1999) Making better 'scents' in anthropology: Aroma in Tuareg sociocultural systems and the shaping of ethnography, *Anthropological Quarterly*, 72 (2): 55–73.

Ribeiro, R. and Collins, H. (2007) The bread-making machine: Tacit knowledge and two types of action, *Organization Studies*, 28 (9): 1417–1433.

Roepstorff (2007) Navigating the brainscape: When knowing becomes seeing, in Grasseni, C. (ed.) *Skilled Visions: Between Apprenticeship and Standards*. Oxford: Berghahn, pp. 191–206.

Samudra, J.K. (2008) Memory in our body: Thick participation and the translation of kinaesthetic experience, *American Ethnologist*, 35 (4): 665–681

Savigliano, M. (1995) *Tango and the Political Economy of Passion*. New York: Routledge.

Schlanger, N. (2006) *Introduction to Mauss, M. (2006) Techniques, Technology and Civilisation* (trans. D. Lussier and J. Redding, ed. N. Schlanger). Oxford: Berghahn, pp. 1–29.

Schröer, N., Hinnenkamp, V., Kreher, S. and Poferl, A. (eds) (2012) *Lebenswelt und Ethnographie*. Essen: Oldib-Verlag.

Schütz, A. (1976) The well informed citizen: An essay on the social distribution of knowledge, in A. Brodersen (ed.) *Collected Papers Volume* II. The Hague: Martinus Nijhoff, pp. 120–134.

Sennett, R. (2008) *The Craftsman*. New Haven, CT: Yale University Press.

Serres, M. (2016) *The Five Senses: A Philosophy of Mingled Bodies*. London: Bloomsbury. (trans. M. Sankey and P. Cowley. Originally published as Les Cinq Sens, Paris: Editions Grasset et Fasquelle, 1985).

Shilling, C. (1997) The undersocialised conception of the embodied agent in modern sociology, *Sociology*, 31 (4): 737–754.

Silverman, D. (2017) How was it for you? The Interview Society and the irresistible rise of the (poorly analyzed) interview, *Qualitative Research*, 17 (2): 144–158.

Solnit, R. (2006) *A Field Guide to Getting Lost*. Edinburgh: Canongate.

Sontag, S. (1977) *On Photography*. New York: Farar, Straus and Giroux.

Stephens, N. and Lewis, J. (2017) Doing laboratory ethnography: Reflections on method in scientific workplaces, *Qualitative Research*, 17 (2): 202–216.

Stephens, N., Glasner, P. and Atkinson, P. (2011) Documenting the doable and doing the documented, *Social Studies of Science*, 41 (6): 791–813.

Stoller, P. (1989) *The Taste of Ethnographic Things: The Senses in Anthropology*. Philadelphia, PA: University of Pennsylvania Press.

Stoller, P. (1997) *Sensuous Scholarship*. Philadelphia, PA: University of Pennsylvania Press.

Streeck, J. and Mehus, S. (2005) Microethnography: The study of practices, in K.L. Fitch and R.E. Sanders (eds) *Handbook of Language and Social Interaction*. Mahwah, NJ: Lawrence Erlbaum.

Sudnow, D. (1978) *Ways of the Hand*. Cambridge, MA: Harvard University Press.

Taussig, M. (2011) *I Swear I Saw This: Drawing in Fieldwork Notebooks, Namely My Own*. Chacago: University of Chicago Press.

Tavory, I. and Timmermans, S. (2014) *Theorizing Qualitative Research*. Chicago: University of Chicago Press.

Teil, G. (1998) Devenir expert aromaticien: Y-a-t-il place pour le goût dans les goûts alimentaires? *Sociologie du Travail*, 98 (4): 503–522.

Terrio, S.J. (2000) *Crafting the Culture and History of French Chocolate*. Berkeley, CA: University of California Press.

Traweek, S. (1988) *Beamtimes and Lifetimes*. Cambridge, MA: Harvard University Press.

Wacquant, E. (2004) *Body and Soul: Notebooks of an Apprentice Boxer*. Oxford: Oxford University Press.

Wacquant, E. (2005) Carnal connections: On embodiment, apprenticeship, and membership, *Qualitative Sociology*, 28, (4): 445–474.

Wellin, C. and Fine, G.A. (2001) Ethnography as work: Career socialization, settings and problems, in P. Atkinson, A. Coffey, S. Delamont, J. Lofland and L. Lofland (eds) *Handbook of Ethnography*. London: SAGE, pp. 323–338.

Whitaker, E. M. and Atkinson, P. (2019a) Authenticity and the interview: a positive response to the radical critique, *Qualitative Research*, 19 (6): 619–634.

Whitaker, E. M. and Atkinson, P. (2019b) Surrender, catch and the imp of fieldwork, *Qualitative Inquiry*, 25 (9-10): 936–944.

Whitaker, E.M. and Atkinson, P. (2021) Reflexive ethnography, in A. Poferl and N. Schröer (eds) *Handbook of Sociological Ethnography*. Wiesbaden: Springer (awaiting publication for page range).

Wolcott, H. F. (2001) *Writing Up Qualitative Research*. 2nd edn. Thousand Oaks, CA: SAGE.

Wong, W.W.Y. (2014) *Van Gogh on Demand: China and the Readymade*. Chicago: University of Chicago Press.

Woodward, S. (2020) *Material Methods: Researching and Thinking with Things*. London: SAGE.

Wrong, D. (1961) The oversocialized conception of man in modern sociology, *American Sociological Review*, 26 (2): 183–193.

Index

www.ingramcontent.com/pod-product-compliance
Lightning Source LLC
Chambersburg PA
CBHW070933030426
42336CB00014BA/2649